THE SON OF THE GOD OF WIND

The Exploits of Śrī Hanumāna

There is no village, town or city where there are no temples dedicated to Śrī Hanumāna jī. Truth is that the spirit of Śrī Hanumāna jī inspires, enlivens and energises the lives of a very large number of people. It motivates them for dedication, piety and service. This book contains stories about Lord Śiva, Śri Rāma, the God of Wind, Kesarī, his wife Añjanā and their son Hanumāna jī.

Pandit Atma Ram Sharma

THE SON OF THE GOD OF WIND

The Exploits of Śrī Hanumāna

New Age Books

New Delhi (India)

THE SON OF THE GOD OF WIND

Published by
NEW AGE BOOKS
A-44, Naraina Industrial Area, Phase-I
New Delhi–110 028 (INDIA)
Email: nab@newagebooksindia.com
Website: www.newagebooksindia.com

ISBN: 978-81-7822-393-3

First Edition: Delhi, 2013

Printed and published by
RP Jain for New Age Books
A-44, Naraina Industrial Area
Phase-1, New Delhi 110 028, India

Publisher's Note

The present work is the result of translation of selected stories about Śrī Hanumāna by late Pandit Atma Ram Sharma, a Sanskrit teacher at Scindia School, Gwalior, Madhya Pradesh. Although the translation is of selected stories only, it makes a coherent and well-connected reading. The translated version was edited by Dr. A.K. Monga. The final reading of the manuscript was done by Dr. G.P. Bhatt who also provided the diacritical marks.

For the Hindus, Hanumāna personifies the highest level of devotion to Lord Rama, an incarnation of Viṣṇu. That is the reason he is held in such high esteem. The book may be of particular interest to non-resident Indians who are always eager to be emotionally connected with their religious and cultural roots.

Unfortunately, Pandit Atma Ram Sharma passed away before the book could see the light of the day. We pay our respects to him and dedicate this book to his memory.

Contents

Introduction

India is a country of the people who are mostly religious. A large chunk of the population worships Hanumāna. There is no village, town or city where there are no temples dedicated to Śrī Hanumāna jī. Truth is that the spirit of Śrī Hanumāna jī inspires, enlivens and energises the lives of a very large number of people. It motivates them for dedication, piety and service. Śrī Hanumāna jī keeps them unwavering on the path of virtue and discipline.

Hanumāna jī has imbibed the nectar of devotion for Śrī Rāma and has ceased to be an entity separate from and independent of Śrī Rāma. He is the embodiment of the qualities which Śrī Rāma personifies in himself. On an occasion he spoke to Śrī Rāma in the following words :

"Lord! From the point of the body I am your servant, from that of life, your part and from that of finality, I am your self."

Śrī Hanumāna jī is very easy to please or propitiate. You repeat the name of Śrī Rāma with a true heart and his devotee, Śrī Hanumāna jī, is present there instantly.

Hanumāna jī is the destroyer of evil. He is very kind and amiable towards the devotees of Lord Rāma. He is an ideal for the people to emulate. He is an embodiment of the qualities of character such as discipline, truthfulness, dedication, unfailing love for the master, righteous living, celibacy and readiness to serve. His devotion to the Lord was the strength of his body and mind. He is the progeny of lady Añjanā but is also called the son of Śaṅkara, the God of Wind and Kesarī.

Hereafter are narrated stories related to Lord Śiva, Lord Rāma, God of Wind, Kesarī, his wife, Añjanā and their son Hanumāna jī.

Who was Añjanā?

In the court of Indra there was a nymph. She was called Puñjalikasthalā. She was extremely charming and frolicsome. Once she ridiculed a sage. The sage could not stand it. He cursed her saying, "As you are frolicking like a monkey, you will become a female monkey."

Hearing the curse, she trembled. She fell at the feet of the sage and begged for mercy. The prayer of the nymph softened the outlook of the sage who, in a mood to pardon her, came down to saying: "Although the curse will not go vain, you will enjoy freedom to assume the form of a woman at will."

The extremely beautiful nymph with extraordinary charming features was born as a daughter to the great majestic Lord of the monkey clan, Kuñjara. Her name was Añjanā. There was no dame on the earth who could equal her in beauty. She was given in marriage to Kesarī. She too was greatly devoted to him. Both lived happily for a long time but were not blessed with a son. The couple lived on the mount Kãncana giri.

Why was Hanumāṇa Born?

The almighty Lord performs playful acts variously. The meditation, contemplation or narration of these acts is a source of unbounded happiness for the devotees. It is auspicious also.

Lord Viṣṇu, the preserver of the creation, had assumed the figure and form of a charming lady when the demons and Gods fell out with each other on the question of distribution of the Ambrosia obtained out of the churning of the ocean. Lord Śiva came to know of it. He adores Lord Viṣṇu in his heart. Knowing about the act of assuming the feminine form, Mohinī, by the Lord Viṣṇu, he became curious to view it. He requested Lord Viṣṇu for the favour of the glimpses of the charms of Mohinī.

Lord Viṣṇu tried to dissuade Him (Lord Śiva), saying that it did not behove Him to view the charms of a feminine figure as He was a yogi and that He had burned kāma deva, Cupid, with the fire of His third eye.

But He, Lord Śiva, continued insisting that He should be favoured with a vision of the Mohinī form.

"Let it be so", replied Lord Viṣṇu and became invisible.

In a moment Lord Śiva found himself in a forest abounding in creepers, plants and trees laden with the wild flowers and leaves of various hues and fragrances. The spring was all around. The bees were buzzing over flowers. The humming birds were balancing themselves in the sky over the flowers and looking for the nectar there.

Suddenly Lord Śiva happened to view a charming damsel playing a ball with her lotus red palms. She was behind the veil of flowering branches of plants. As a drop of the ocean of the divinity is more beautiful than the beauty of the creation, Lord Śiva, who had at a point of time burnt to ash cupid, was now unable to restrain his senses from watching the damsel playing with a ball. Suddenly a draught of cool breeze ruffled her attire and she was perceived in nudity by Lord Śiva. He could not hold himself up. The damsel tried to hide herself behind a grove. Lord Śiva shamelessly rushed towards her; His spouse, Umā, His Gaṇas, Gods and sages were watching the scenario in amazement. None came forward to bring him to his senses. The unsuccessful lust converts itself into anger. Who could afford to face the fire of the anger of Lord Śiva? All were imbecile. Finally the virility of the Lord precipitated into a climax. Now the Lord returned to senses and realised the height of the situation. He prayed and prayed to the illusory power of Lord Viṣṇu to grace him with the vision of the truth. Having come down to senses, He set out for Kailāśa, his abode.

The virility of the Lord could not go in vain. He motivated the seven sages to make its use for the promotion of the object of the incarnation of Śrī Rāma. They placed the material on a leaf and induced it into the body of Añjanā through the passage of the ear. Thus was born Śrī Hanumāna.

Añjanā lived with her husband happily for a long time. Yet she was not blessed with a son. In order to have one she practised severe penances.

The sage Mataṅga on seeing her practising severe penances went to her and asked about the reason for that severity.

Añjanā offered her obeisance at the feet of the sage Mataṅga and apprised him of her desire for a son. She said, "O great among the sages, Kesarī the illustrious in the clan of monkeys, beseeched my father for my hand. He wedded me to him. I have been living with him for quite some time but without the blessing of a son. For this I performed and observed many fasts and penances but in vain. Saddened by my fate, I have resolved to undergo severity of penances of life. O great among the Brahmanas, enlighten me, please, on the method of having an illustrious son of an unparalleled repute."

Mataṅga, who commanded an enormous wealth of penances, told her to go to the mount of Veṅkaṭa and worship at his feet there. He also told her that He vouchsafes His devotees with their wishes of the worldly bliss and emancipation. He advised her to go to the bank of Akāśagaṅgā for a dip later.

The river was not far away from there. Having said this he counselled her further to propitiate the God of Wind, "You will be blessed with a son whom the Gods, the demons and the humans will not be able to humiliate in a battle or with the weapons," he prophesied.

Añjanā offered her obeisance at the feet of the great sage. Later she journeyed to Mount Veṅkaṭa. There she worshipped the feet of Veṅkaṭa. As a suffix to the performance, she bathed in the holy water of Akāśagaṅgā, drank it and to propitiate the God of Wind began to observe the most severe penances with all the austerity at her command. She performed penances with full faith, dedication and perseverance, caring little for the pains of the body. Her performance remained unbroken.

The Sun God was in aries. The full Moon was on chitra. Pleased with the severity of her penances, the Lord of the Wind appeared and told her to ask for a boon.

Seeing the deity in person before her, she felt gratified. She touched His feet with her forehand and, hands folded, expressed her aspiration saying, "Lord bless me with a son who would be the best in all the times." The propitiated Lord of Wind said, "O beautiful, I will come to you as your son and grace you with renown and glory in the entire creation."

On being favoured with the boon, Añjanā felt happy beyond bounds. Receiving the news of the gratification of his dear spouse with a boon, Kesarī, the king of the monkey clan, felt extremely joyous.

Once it happened that the most beautiful, large-eyed Añjanā bedecked herself. She donned a yellow saree. It aborned her beautiful person. The fringe of the saree was red. She decorated herself with the ornaments of heavenly flowers of various hues and fragrances. She was looking the divine beauty in person.

Añjanā was standing on a peak of the mountain. She was appreciating the beauty of the nature. She was musing within; at that time a desire for a virtuous son arose in her heart. What a satisfying thing it would have been, had she had a baby son.

All of a sudden a gush of wind ruffled her attire slightly. Her person became visible. She felt as if somebody had touched her person.

The virtuous Añjanā became nervous. She adjusted her dress, scolded the insolence of the invisible being saying, "who dared touch my person and violate my vow of single minded unfaltering love for my husband?" She was on the verge of cursing him.

Seeing Añjanā furious, the Lord of Wind appeared before her.

He said, "O renowned for glory, I do not intend to violate your vow of single minded love for your husband. Do not be apprehensive. Invisibly I have embraced you and with the power of unfaltering will I have favoured you with a son who will be exalted in perseverance, fierceness, power and valor. No one will match him in calibre."

Añjanā felt exuberant. She pardoned the Lord of Wind. She became pregnant. In course of time, happiness of Kesarī knew no bounds.

King Daśaratha, the great one in the line of Raghu, though advanced in age, felt extremely morose as he was not blessed with a child till then. On the advice of the sage Vaśiṣtha, he got a sacrificial prayer performed by the sage Riṣyaśriṅga to beget a son. The prayer was called putreṣṭi which would fulfil an aspiration for a son. The king offered prayers with full faith and hope. Propitiated with the performance, the

Fire God appeared with an urn of milk pudding in his hands. He gave the urn to the king and said that his wish was granted. He advised him to distribute the pudding among his wives. The Fire God then disappeared.

The king gave half of the share to his senior wife Kauśalyā. The remaining portion was again divided into two shares. Both the shares were placed at the hands of Kauśalyā and Kaikeyī. With the approval of Kauśalyā, they were given to Kaikeyī and Sumitrā. Kaikeyī with her share of pudding in her hand was thinking absent mindedly for a while when a female vulture unexpectedly whizzed down and snatching her share, whirled away into the sky. Kaikeyī felt greatly disappointed. Then Kauśalyā and Sumitrā parted with some amount out of their share and gave it to Kaikeyī. The three queens became pregnant in course of time. Kauśalyā was blessed with the baby Śrī Rāma Candra, Kaikeyī with Bharata and Sumitrā with Laxmaṅa and Satrughna.

Kesarī, the king of the monkey race, was living on the mount Sumeru with his charming wife Añjanā. She had practised severe penances for seven thousand years and worshipped Śiva, the spouse of Umā. Thus propitiated, Śiva told her to ask for a boon. She prayed for a worthy son who would be the embodiment of virtue and calibre.

The Lord, who is easy to propitiate, spoke to her, "One of the eleven Rudras, my eleventh and the fierce form, will be born to you as a son. You take a *mantra*, a seed word, from me. You repeat it. The God of Wind will bless you with the oblation. On account of that you will become a mother and get a son. He will be endowed with all the qualities and calibre." The spouse of Umā disappeared.

Añjanā began repeating the *mantra*. While repeating the *mantra* she kept her palms joined in a posture of begging. At that very point of time, the female vulture carrying the Kaikeyī's share of pudding passed over her. The body of the female vulture shrank and the cup of the pudding fell from her beak. The Wind God was ready for it. He let it fall into the palms of Añjanā. Lord Śiva had already apprised her of it. She at once accepted the pudding reverently and became pregnant.

The Birth of Hanumāna

It was the auspicious full moon of Caitra. The day was Tuesday. At this auspicious juncture of time, Lord Śiva, his eleventh Rudra form, the fierce and the violent, in order to see and associate Himself in the playful acts of Śrī Rāma, whom he adores in his heart, was born to Añjanā as her son, Hanumāna, on the earth. He is also taken as the son of the God of Wind. He is the bravest of the brave and worthiest of the worthy.

Some hold that he was born on the eleventh day of the white aspect of Caitra, under the star Māgha. Others say that he was born on the fourteenth day of the black aspect of Kārtika. There is another school which believes that he was born on the full moon of that month.

According to some Tuesday is the day of his birth, others say Saturday is the day of his birth. For the ostentatious devouts of Hanumāna, all the days are auspicious.

When Hanumāna, the incarnation of the eleventh form of Rudra, the violent and the fierce, the son of the God of the Wind, the son of Kesarī, the blissful son of Añjanā, had put his foot on the earth, the entire nature wore a charming look. All the quarters were pleasant. The rays of the Sun were gentle and pleasing. Clear water flowed in the rivers. The mountains awaited the arrival of the son of Añjanā. The waterfalls were exuberant with freshness. The pleasing flowers of various hues were blooming in the garden and sending forth their fragrances all around. The bees were buzzing over and around them. The breeze was waving gently everywhere, as if under the influence of joy.

Lord Śaṅkara appeared as a son to Añjanā. At the time of his birth, his charms were beyond comparison and description. The glow of his body at that time was red-brown or golden yellow. His eyes and hair too were of the same complexion. He was born with the rings of the same colour on his ears. He was donning a cap on his head. It was studded with gems. He was donning a small length of cloth over his privities.

The sacred thread adorned his chest. He was holding the destructive weapon of thunderbolt in one hand. On his loin he was sporting a girdle of Mūnja, the sacred grass. Seeing the beauty of her son, mother Añjanā felt ecstatic.

When Hanumāna put his foot down on the earth, it felt that it was immensely fortunate. The joy of mother Añjanā and father Kesarī, the king of the monkey clan, knew no bounds. The waves of joy reverberated all around. The Gods, the sages, the monkeys, the mountains, the waterfalls, the lakes, the rivers, the oceans, the beasts, the birds and not only the living and non-living, but also the mother earth were all abounding in the joyousness. The splendour of the joyous feeling prevailed in the entire creation and made it a Kingdom of bliss.

The Childhood of Hanumāna

Añjanā reared her son with great affection and care. She loved him more than her life. Kesarī, the king of monkeys, also loved him immensely. When the baby Hanumāna would coo, shriek or scream out of joy, the hearts of the mother Añjanā and father Kearī would brim with ecstasy. The playful activities of the child Hanumāna were not only delightful but also unique.

Once it so happened, Kesarī was out somewhere. Mother Añjanā also, leaving him (Hanumāna) in the cradle, had gone out in the forest to gather fruits and flowers. The baby Hanumāna felt hungry. In the absence of the mother he began shrieking, agitating his hands and feet briskly. Suddenly his eyes fell on the eastern horizon. The Sun was rising. He mistook the disk of the Sun for a red fruit.

Age is not a condition for brilliance and heroism. And here in the lap of Añjanā, the eleventh Rudra himself, the fierce and the terrible, who annihilates the creation, was sporting as Hanumāna. The God of Wind had already bequeathed him with the ability to fly. Hanumāna ejected himself out of the cradle and began flying in the sky with the velocity and the strength of the wind. He was flying in the sky with speed and force. The Gods, the demons and the yakṣas were watching in amazement and saying that even the wind, Garuda and the mind do not command such a speed as he, the son of the God of Wind in infancy does. If he is so heroic and terrible at this age, what power will he command when he attains adulthood?

The God of Wind viewed his son advancing towards the sun. He felt worried and anxious. "My son may not scorch himself with the fiery rays of the Sun." For this reason he began accompanying him in a state of cool air, as cool as the ice.

The Sun saw a divine child advancing towards himself. He took no time to realise that the son of the God of Wind was coming towards him with the speed of his father, and the God of Wind too was coming with him to protect him. The Sun thought the Lord Śiva himself, who adorns the moon in his locks, was coming to him as Hanumāna, and felt immensely fortunate. He cooled his fiery rays down. Hanumāna climbed onto the chariot of the Sun and began playing with him. The juncture was that it was the day on which the moon is invisible. Rāhu, the son of Simhika, came onto the chariot of the Sun to swallow him. Then he viewed the child Hanumāna askance. Not taking his presence into account, he advanced to engulf the Sun. Hardly had he closed on to him, Śri Hanumāna jī caught hold of him. Caught in the clenched fist, he began screaming. The grip of the fist was terrible. He began to struggle for his life. Somehow he escaped from the deadly grip of Śri Hanumāna jī and ran straight up to the presiding God of Gods, Indra, and wailed before him. There in despair and anger he cried that he had been provided with the Sun and the Moon as the means of satiating his hunger. He wanted the reason why he had been shorn of his right and somebody else endowed with it. He spoke with his brows twitched in anger.

Hearing the presentation of Rāhu, the son of Simhika, Indra gasped in amazement. He further stated that, that being the day of festival, "I had hardly reached the Sun to have my usual nibble, when I encountered another Rahu who gripped me fiercly. Somehow I saved my life and reached here."

Indra saw that Rāhu was quite angry. His eyes were brimming with tears. Indra felt anxious, rose up, mounted his elephant, Airāvata, and proceeded towards the site of the event, Rahu preceeding him. The spouse of Śachi was at a loss of his wits to comprehend the presence of such a hero, so close to the enemy of the darkness as could frighten Rahu away from him.

There Rāhu rushed towards the Sun. Seeing him, Śrī Hanumāna remembered his hunger; taking him for an attractive food, pounced over him.

Rāhu, shouting for help and protection rushed towards Indra, who ran to protect him. On the escape of Rāhu, Śrī Hanumāna mistook Airāvat for a tasty eat. He sprang upon it. At that time Śrī Hanumāna was looking brilliant and fierce as the fire aflame. Indra was terror stricken. He hurled his weapon of bolt on the child. It afflicted Śrī Hanumāna on the left aspect of his chin. It fractured. In grief he fell unconscious. Seeing his lovely and dear son screaming and crumbling for life, the God of Wind was angry with Indra and in fury held up the movement of winds. He entered a cave with his son on his lap, with the result that the course of breathing of all the living beings in all the worlds came to a halt, the joints of their parts and limbs began to crack. They all were stilled like wood. Acts of Dharma also came to a halt. In a frenzy, the terrified Indra, the Gods of Gandharvas, the demons, the serpents and the guhyakas, the guardians of the treasures of Kubera, approached Brahmā, the creator, with a prayer to save life, who, alongwith all of them, reached the cave where the God of Wind, with his son held to his chest, was shedding tears in grief. The four-faced Brahmā beholding the unconscious child glowing like the Sun, the fire and the gold, was amazed.

Viewing the creator in front of him, the God of Wind, with Hanumāna on his lap, stood up in reverence for him. At that time the celestial rings on ears of Hanumāna were waving. The coronet on his head, the string of pearls on the chest and the divine ornaments of gold on his person were exquisitely shining. The God of Wind fell at the feet of Brahmā. The four-faced God lifted him up lovingly and solaced his son affectionately. The unconsciousness of Śrī Hanumāna jī disappeared at the gentle touch of him who is born out of the lotus. He rose to sit up. Seeing that his son was alive, the God of Wind, who is the life of all living beings, began blowing as before. The living beings regained their lives then.

Satisfied, Brahmā jī, granted a boon to him and said that this child would never be subjected to a curse by a brāhmana and that no part of his body would ever suffer an affliction with a weapon.

Later, addressing the congregation of the Gods there he said, "the child would render a great service to them all and that they should invest him with boons."

Indra, the God of Gods, heard this and pleased immensely on the occasion, said that as the chin of this child was affected with the weapon Vajra shot by him, he will be called Hanumāna and that his body would get the strength that would not allow his weapon Vajra to penetrate it and that it would grow stronger than his Vajra itself. He also honoured him with a garland of lotuses, which would never fade.

The Sun God, who was present there, offered a hundredth part of his brilliance to him, besides this he offered to make him well versed in the knowledge of scriptures saying that their essence would reveal itself to him and that he would be an erudite orator of unmatched calibre.

Varuna vouchsafed that the child would always be saved against the impact of the noose and the net wielded by him.

Yama said that the boy would enjoy eternal health and immortality.

Kubera, who is gold yellow and heads the clan of Yakṣas, blessed him with safety against the mace and immunity against sorrow. Also that the Yakṣas and Rākṣasas would never be able to surmount him in battles.

Lord Śaṅkara granted him immunity against his weapons.

Viśwakarma granted him eternal security against the divine weaponry invented by him and also immortality.

There the Gods had invested him with the boons which would never fail him. Lord Brahmā, not feeling satisfied with this much, further blessed him with deathlessness against his infallible missile. Overwhelmed with joy he further blessed him with sainthood and longevity that would never come to an end.

Addressing Māruti he later said that this son of hers would perpetuate terror on the foes and immunity from peril for friends. He will enjoy immortal fame. He will perform the deeds which would be unique and which would cause a thrill of joy or horror.

Having invested him with boons and blessings, the Gods and demigods departed for their respective abodes.

Curse from the Sages

The child Hanumāna was very restless and naughty. Firstly, he was Śaṅkara incarnate, who annihilates the creation, secondly a monkey child and over that, blessed by Gods with unfailing boons. His playful acts would please his parents. To swing the lion by its tail, to test the power of an elephant by holding its trunk and pulling it in the opposite direction were his usual plays. He would shake a giant tree by its roots. He would jump over a mount from a mount and reach anywhere. All the impregnable forests and ranges in the vicinity had been mapped by him.

The wild creatures feared him but loved him inwardly. He was the friend and saviour of all the living beings. He would not tolerate any tormentor of the weak. Hopping from the top of a tree to that of another, he would go far. He would lighten his weight if he feared that a branch of a tree would break under it.

Endowed as he was with unique power, invested upon him by the Gods as boons and blessings, he would reach the hermitages and would annoy the hermits there. He would place the seat of a hermit near somebody else. He would wrap himself with the deer skin and hop over to the top of a tree. Or he would hang the deer skin on a higher branch of a tree. He would empty the water jar of a hermit, hurl it on the ground and break it or throw it away into a river.

He would sit on the top of a meditating ascetic or devotee repeating the name of God. The sages would observe the promise of non-violence and he would pull the beard violently and run away. He would hold the cloth or the sacred book of recitation and enchantment in his hands and teeth, tear it and throw it away. He would hold the sacrificial utensil such as wooden ladle in his hands and break it. He would tear the garments of the bark which the hermits gathered after great pains. Knowing that he had been blessed with very powerful and infallible boons by Gods, they would keep quiet but they all felt very sad and agitated. Their agony was real and immense.

Gradually he came of age to study but his restive nature went on. His parents also grew anxious. They tried to persuade their lovely son to the behaviour of quietude but in vain. His idiosyncrasies continued as before. Frustrated in their effort, Añjanā and Kesarī approached the sages. They narrated their tale of woe and suffering. They beseeched the sages thus, "You have gathered the wealth of penances. We got this child after severe penances, as a blessing. Please have mercy on him in such a way that he acquires learning and knowledge. His temperament can evolve only as a grace of your mercy. We humbly entreat you to condescend on us."

The sages contemplated, "This child is aware of his power and strength. If he forgets them, he will improve himself really."

Some ascetics, who were advanced in penances and had attained an insight, realized that the child was to deliver good to the cause of Gods. He would be a resolute devotee to Śrī Rāma and for an ostentatious devout the egoistic awareness of power and strength was not good. Service to the Lord only with humility is desirable. For this reason the sages of the clan of Bhṛgu and Aṅgirā cursed Hanumāna thus, "O brave among the monkeys! You will forget for long time the power and strength on account of which you have been agonising us so far. The curse from us would turn you unaware of your power. Reminded by somebody, you will regain your power and strength."

Cursed in this way, the son of the God of Wind, was deprived of his power and strength. He began to behave as a humble and polite child. His brilliant fierceness and heroism came down to a low level. Like other children of the monkey race, he too went round the hermitages quietly. The sages too felt pleased at this change to humility and politeness.

Education by the Mother

The mother's way of living and her teachings create the deepest impression on the life and personality of the child. The ideal mothers mould their sons in such a way that they grow into great and ideal beings. History and the Purāṇas are full of such examples.

Añjanā, the mother of Sri Hanumāna jī, a great lady of noble character, had the merit of austerity and the wealth of virtue. She had observed severe penances with devotion and a resolute mind. With the same dedication and awareness, she devoted herself to the shaping of the life and character of her son who was dearer to her than her own life. Seeing the heroic deeds of Hanumāna jī, she used to feel ecstatic in her heart and would encourage him to follow the path of bravery and heroism.

She would narrate the tales from the Purāṇas to her dear son after the obligatory observance of the religious rite and before retiring to bed at night. Time and again she would narrate the stories of the models to her son and would remind him of their noble deeds and qualities of character. She would also question him what he would imbibe and emulate from these examples. What is concealed and obscure from the sight of the Lord Śiva? (Hanumāna jī is an incarnation of the Lord Śiva.) Lord Śiva is omniscient and dwells in every heart. But in a playful mood Hanumāna jī would behave as an ignorant being and would answer wrongly. The mother would correct the child and fix the correct answer in his mind. All the stories of the incarnations of the almighty, the ocean of mercy, were on the tip of the tongue of Śrī Hanumāna jī. He used to relate those stories to his fellows and friends with love and gusto.

When Añjanā initiated the narration of the story of incarnation of Śrī Rāma, Hanumāna would converge all his attention on it. Lethargy or sluggishness would never come to his mind. When the mother would feel sleepy, Hanumāna jī would wake her up and ask, "Mother! what next?"

The mother would begin again. Hanumāna jī's love for the story was insatiable. He would request his mother again and again to relate the story of the Lord Rāma. She would tell him the story and he would go into ecstasy. His eyes would brim with tears, his body parts would flourish with energy. He would sally into imagining, "Had I been that Hanumāna...."

In the course of the story the mother Añjanā would ask, "Son! would you be like that Hanumāna?"

Hanumāna jī's answer would always be, "Yes, mother I would certainly become that Hanumāna. But where are Śrī Rāma and Rāvaṇa? If Rāvaṇa would cast an evil eye on the mother Sīta jī, I would crush him to nullity."

Añjanā would continue, "Son! You are that Hanumāna. Rāvaṇa is reigning over Laṅkā even today. Rāma is born as a son to Daśaratha, the king of Ayodhyā. You grow into a full person soon. Power and strength are required for assisting Rāma in his endeavors. You become strong and enterprising without losing time."

"Mother! I am not fragile," with these words uttered he would jump down his bed and flourishing his biceps, he would show up to her as a proof of his valour. Mother Añjanā would smile and embracing him close to her bosom, would sing glory to Śrī Rāma and pat him to sleep. Hanumāna jī too clinging to her bosom would go to sleep soon in the warmth of her love and affection. Hanumāna jī's fondness for the story of Śrī Rāma was spontaneous . He would listen to it time and again. Each time he listened to the story of Rāma, he contemplated on his heroic deeds and exploits. As a result the cord binding him with Śrī Rāma grew thicker and stronger with the passage of time. Gradually greater amount of his time got utilised in the meditation on Śrī Rāma. He would sit in trance some times in the cave of a mount, some times on the bank of a river and some times in a dense grove of plants and shrubs. In the course of the trance, tears of love would roll down his cheeks. Due to his absorption in meditation he would lose awareness of the natural urges like hunger and thirst. Mother Añjanā, feeling anxious for him, the lovable part of her being, would roam the forests, the mountains, river banks and waterfalls in search for him, every noon and afternoon to feed him. She would bring him home after a long exercise and then after a great exertion would succeed in making him accept a morsel or two of food. This became the usual daily routine of Śrī Hanumāna jī. He was so deeply absorbed in meditation on his revered idol that he lost awareness of his body. He would be absorbed in the chanting of the words Rāma-Rāma and only Rāma-Rāma all the time.

Instruction from the Sun

Seeing the state of her son, Añjanā sometimes felt sad. Kesarī, the king of the monkey clan, felt anxious all the time. Hanumāna had now attained the schooling age. The parents now thought that he should be sent to a guru for instructions. This might be a change for better. Although they were aware of the boons bestowed upon their son by the Gods, Brahmā and others, they knew that the great souls do not act freely and that they do not violate the established norms of the conduct in social life. They knew that their son was knowledge and virtue personified. Still they felt that he should go to a guru and abide by the traditions pursued by the great divine souls. They always follow the rules set by the scriptures and never deviate from the path of righteousness. In spite of being knowledge and virtue personified, they go to the preceptors for schooling and serve them with humility. Serving them with devotion and faith, receive, imbibe and emulate what they learn with them. Truth is that knowledge acquired with humility and dedication blossoms into fruition. With this in their mind they decided to send Hanumāna to the residence of a guru for education. With a great joy they performed the investiture ceremony of Hanumāna and allowed him to go to a guru for initiation into the learning of the Vedas. But, who was the guru? Who was the embodiment of all the qualities, which are to be sought in a guru? Where to find such a guru? These were the questions, which were agitating the mind of the parents of Śrī Hanumāna jī.

Mother Añjanā besought him, "Son, the Sun God witnesses the whole world. All the subtleties of the scriptures are clear to him. He has promised to educate you when the suitable time arrives. Therefore, you approach him and learn the scriptures with humility, faith and devotion."

Śrī Hanumāna jī, wearing the loin rope of the mūñja grass, a narrow strip of cloth and the sacred thread on his shoulder, looked towards the Sun God and began contemplating. Mother Añjanā knew about the curse from the sages. She at once reminded him, "Son, the Sun God is not beyond your reach. Your powers know no bounds. He is that Sun God whom you had mistaken for a ripe fruit and had reached to swallow him. You have played with him. Even Indra was overawed by your presence there. Dear, there is no job which you cannot accomplish; nothing is impossible for you. You go, reach the Sun God, beseech him for the real knowledge and receive it. Your welfare is certain!"

Instantly Śrī Hanumāna jī got ready within, touched the feet of the mother and the father and obtained their blessing. Next moment he hopped and encountered Aruṇa, the charioteer of the Sun. Hanumāna jī mentioned the name of his father. Aruna admitted him into the audience of the Sun.

Hanumāna jī very politely and humbly offered his obeisance at his feet. Seeing him, the son of the God of Wind, politeness personified, simplicity incarnate, generosity embodied, standing, folded hands, the Sun enquired about the reason for his presence there.

Hanumāna jī responded in a very sweet and soft voice, "Lord! After investiture ceremony, my mother ordained me to reach you for knowledge. I beseech you to oblige me."

The Sun said, "To have a student like you would be a source of joy for any teacher. I would be more than happy to have you as my pupil. But you see my peculiar position. I have to course the time and the space every moment. This Aruṇa, my charioteer, does not know how to slacken the speed. Unmindful of hunger and thirst, he goes on speeding my vehicle. I have no right to complain to the creator in this respect. It is not possible for me to alight from the chariot.

Under these circumstances how shall I be able to teach you? You think about it and tell me what should be done. You are an ideal boy and I would feel happy to have you as my pupil. But these are my limitations."

The Sun tried to dissuade him. But, the son of the God of Wind did not perceive any difficulty in it. With the same politeness he insisted, "The speed of the chariot would not present any obstruction in the course of my learning. Of course it should not present any inconvenience to you. I will sit in front of you and will advance with the speed of the chariot. My learning too will go on unhindered with the speed of the vehicle."

The son of the God of Wind was facing the destroyer of the darkness.

The Sun did not have an iota of surprise in it. He was aware of the power of the son of the wind. He also knew that the child was the foremost among the erudite. In order to keep the tradition of the scriptures and to grace him (the Sun) with credit, he had approached him with a request for education.

The Sun was uttering the Vedas, the scriptures, the disciplines, their links and sublinks as fast as he could and Śrī Hanumāna jī was imbibing all that with rapt attention and with no interruption. The questions and answers, the doubts and their resolutions were not required at all. Not in the course of years or months but in a few days he explained all the Vedas, the scriptures, sub-scriptures and all their branches. The entire knowledge was already present in him, in a living state naturally. The process of imparting knowledge culminated into its enlivenment. He reached the end of all knowledge.

With deep devotion to the preceptor, he lay prostrate at his feet and entreated him for allowing him to offer to him fee or some present for the knowledge received. He said, "Please enlighten me as to what I may offer at your feet now, at the completion of the period of my studentship."

The Sun God was free of desires. He answered, "If you promise to extend the protection to Sugrīva, the younger brother of Bālī, I shall be pleased immensely. He was born out of a part of mine."

"I shall obey your command. Me remaining unscathed, no power on earth will ever be able to hurt Sugrīva. I give my word," Śrī Hanumāna vowed.

The Sun God blessed him, "May you be blessed in all ways."

Hanumāna jī lay prostrate at the feet of his preceptor again.

The erudite Hanumāna, the son of the God of Wind, returned to the mount Gandhmadana, and put his forehead at the feet of his mother and the father. Their joy knew no bounds. They celebrated the arrival of their son. There was festivity and rejoicing. The celebration was elaborate and grand. No one had ever seen before such an observance on the mount. The whole monkey clan rejoiced in ecstasy. All blessed the mother Añjanā, from the core of their heart.

With the Child Rāma

Lord Śiva is camphor-fair. Śrī Rāma is blue complexioned. Truth is that Lord Śiva and Śrī Rāma are essentially one and the same. There is no duality between the two. Therefore, those who revere Śrī Govinda, revere Śrī Śiva too. Those who adore Śrī Hari intensely, they worship Lord Śiva also. Those who affront Śiva, the variegated eyed, offend the Lord Vishnu, the agitator of men. Those who do not know the truth of Rudra, do not understand Keśava too.

Lord Śiva Himself said, "Those who perceive the unmanifest Vishnu and me, the Mahadeva, as one, are not re-born. But, in order to enjoy their playful acts, they the Śiva, thc Asutosa, thc one who is easy to propitiate and He who enchants to the hearts of the sages, both are born as Śrī Rāma."

Śrī Rāma destroys the agony caused by the sins. He establishes the dharma, the piety. He assures goodness, peace and auspiciousness in entirety for all the people. When Śrī Rāma is born on the earth to accomplish these ends, Lord Śiva also assumes body to witness the playful acts of Śrī Rāma. Lord Śiva adores Śrī Rāma in his heart. His playful acts charm the entire creation and bestow auspiciousness upon the whole creation. Lord Śiva associates himself in His mission through his partial incarnation. He also enjoys Himself viewing His charming playful acts. Then his ecstasy knows no bounds.

Śrī Rāma, the purifier of the world, was born to the fortunate lady Kauśalyā. Śiva, the spouse of Umā, too began roaming the lanes and paths of the Ayodhyā. He would appear at the gates of Daśaratha and ask for alms. Sometimes he would come as a devout singer of the virtues of the almighty. Sometimes he would assume the role of an erudite pandit and narrate the exploits and the heroic deeds of the various incarnations of the almighty. Sometimes he would assume the role of a fortune teller and would offer to foretell the effects of planetary conjunctions in the horoscope of Śrī Rāma and, reaching closer to him, would love to lift Him up on his lap. On some pretext or the other, he would come closer to him to enjoy his proximity. As a palmist he would love the feel of softness of the palm of his adorable deity. He would show off as the one who knows all the three phases of the being—the past, the present and the future. The lotus eyes of the Lord Rāma had unique charm and would enthrall any viewer. So did they Śiva. Sometimes he would dust the lotus feet of the Lord Rāma with the locks of his hair. Sometimes he would feel and sense the red soft lotus feet of his Lord with the lashes of his eyes. The pleasure of feeling the feet of Śrī Rāma was beyond the reach of even Gods. He would touch, stroke, feel and sense them variously and experience the state of bliss which is beyond the reach of yogins and even Gods.

With the passage of time Śrī Rāma, the source of the joy for the members of the family of Raghu, began to reach the door of the palace.

Once it so happened that the spouse of the daughter of the loftiest and the greatest among the mountains, the Himālaya, appeared there at the door of the palace, in the guise of a monkey charmer. He had a beautiful monkey who would dance to the tune or beats played by the charmer. The children of Ayodhya flocked around him.

The charmer began playing the drum. Shortly after, the four brothers including Śrī Rāma, arrived at the door. The charmer beat the drum and the monkey folded its hands.

Śrī Rāma alongwith his brothers laughed. The monkey charmer felt fulfilled. He began beating the drum more vigorously. The monkey began dancing to the beats. By one partial incarnation, Lord Śiva was dancing in front of him whom he adores in his heart. By another aspect, he himself was making him dance. The one who was dancing and He who was making the one dance, were the same one supreme being, the spouse of Pāravatī, the devout of the lotus feet of Śrī Rāma. The one who was enjoying the dance and clapping his hands, was the son of Kauśalya, Śrī Rāma himself, who makes the entire creation dance like a dancer. Śrī Rāma is the Lord of the whole world.

In the end Śrī Rāma felt immensely pleased and insisted to have that monkey. He expressed his desire saying, "I want this monkey."

Rāma, the eldest son of the sovereign of the world, yearns for something and the yearning cannot go unfulfilled. The charmer may demand any amount of money as the price but the monkey would remain with the son of Kauśalya. The charmer also desired this. He had come to the door of his lord only to submit and surrender himself at his feet. (The monkey was the Lord Śiva incarnate.) Śrī Rāma accepted the monkey in his lotus like hands. The monkey too was longing for the meeting and it had been going unfulfilled for the ages; this was fulfilled today. He began dancing. Till now Bholānātha, the lord of simplicity, was making his own form, the eleventh Rudra, as the monkey, dance, but now He himself, the embodiment of simplicity, was dancing. The power, which was inspiring him to dance, was Śrī Rāma, the son of the king Dasaratha. Śrī Rāma is the swan sporting in the lake of the hearts of the sages. The happiness, the fortune and the ecstasy of the monkey knew no bounds today. He was expressing his inner sentiments through all kinds of gestures there in the presence of Śrī Rāma, the child, and his charmer became invisible in a moment. Not noticed by others, he had reached the mount Kailāśa. In order to witness the playful acts of his master He had entered His other form.

Thus Śrī Hanumāna jī got the opportunity to live near his master Śrī Rāma, the child Rāma. Śrī Rāma loved Hanumāna jī immensely. He would squat beside him, play with him, caress his body of the golden hue, would ask him to dance and would send him running to bring something from a distance. Hanumāna jī would obey all his comands swiftly with a sense of honour. He would feel gratified and happy. He would please him in every way. He would do only that which would entertain him, please him or make him happy.

Many years passed as if in half a moment. The sage Viśvāmitra arrived at Ayodhyā. When the time to leave approached, he, Śrī Rāma called Hanumāna jī aside and apprised him thus, "My closest companion Hanumāna my main mission of the incarnation on the earth is to begin now. The life on the earth is in turmoil because of evil deeds and immoral ways of Ravana. Now the time has come to finish him and establish the kingdom of Dharma, virtue, on the earth. This mission of mine will require your assistance. Rāvaṇa is in league with Bālī. He is after the blood of his younger brother Sugrīva. Terrified Sugrīva is living on the mount Riṣyamūka. Therefore you go there and make friends with him. In the vicinity there live Mārīca, Subāhu and Tādkā. I will slay and emancipate them soon. This much done, I will enter Danḍkāraṇya soon. There I will clear the terrible thorns like Khara, Dūsaṇa, Triśirā and Śūrpaṇakhā in a few days. There you prepare the bridge of friendship between Sugrīva and me. Then you help me in my mission with the assistance of the monkeys and bears."

Hanumāna jī did not like the separation from his master. But the submission to the commands of the master is the supreme duty for him. He offered his obeisance at the feet of his master and set out on the journey to the mount Ṛiṣyamūka. He was repeating the sweet names of his master within. His names are the source of the good and the auspicious.

Secretary to Sugrīva

Ṛkṣarajā was from the monkey clan. He had two sons—Bālī and Sugrīva. As a father, he loved both the sons equally. Both were intelligent, wise, handsome, powerful, strong and courageous. Both loved each other immensely. Bālī loved Sugrīva as his own self and Sugrīva revered his elder brother as his father. Both were together in eating, sleeping, playing and in hunting. Mostly they moved together.

After the death of their father, the ministers crowned the elder brother as the sovereign of the monkey clan. The whole monkey clan held him in high esteem and love and he too loved his people as his own offspring. In this way Bālī ruled over the vast kingdom of Kiṣkindhā and Sugrīva, on account of being faithful and docile by nature, remained in the service of his elder brother.

Besides this, Kesarī, alongwith his wife, Añjanā, felt extremely anxious as to the indrawn tendencies and detached nature of Hanumāna. He was a commander of a troop of the monkeys and functioned under the command of Ṛksaraja. In order that Hanumāna acquires the knowledge of polity he deputed him to Pampāpura. Hanumāna revered his parents as deities. As soon as he heard the command, he touched their feet and having been blessed, he left on the journey to Pampāpura.

Hearing that Hanumāna had arrived at Pampāpura, Sugrīva went up to welcome him. Bālī was aware of his qualities and also of the fact that those were the rare ones even with the Gods. Bālī extended a hearty respect to him and kept him at his close quarters. Hanumāna was learned, brave, wise and courageous. Bālī desired to cultivate a close friendship with him. But he never forgot his promise which he had given to his preceptor, the Sun God. For this reason he became a close friend of Sugrīva. Sugrīva too had a very soft corner for him.

At the time of Hanumāna's arrival at Pampāpur, it was surrounded by the demon kingdoms all round. On one side were powerful Khara and Dūṣaṇa, on the other was Virādha and on the third side Rāvaṇa had his kingdom. He was the enemy of Gods and Brāhmanas. There was none to dispute or challenge his authority. Bālī was a brave warrior of rare calibre. The demons feared him. They had no courage to create trouble on the boundaries of his kingdom. Being aware of their evil nature and their proximity, he could not have a free time to sojourn at some place, far or near. He could not go beyond his kingdom to crush his enemies even. But with the arrival of Hanumāna at Pampāpura, Bālī's anxiety about the demonic enemies came to an end. Mother Añjanā had related many stories of the demons and their evil tempers to her divine son in his infancy and childhood. He had developed disgust and anger for demonic ways. It was next to impossible that a demon comes near him and goes unscathed. He would go out in search for them, find them and do away with them. The very name of Hanumāna, its mere mention, would send a wave of terror in their hearts and they, apprehending his presence somewhere or anywhere in the neighbourhood, would flee the place without losing time.

Bālī had developed a very soft corner for Hanumāna. He appreciated his simplicity, courage, valour and humility, most of all.

Bālī and Sugrīva were the loving brothers. Both loved each other immensely. But the destiny had different designs.

Once Māyāvī, the youthful son of the demon Māyā, arrived at Kiṣkindhā. He roared at the gate of the town. The time was midnight. Bālī, the brave, was fast asleep in his chamber. Hearing the roar of challenge, he left the bed at once and ran out of the palace to see who dared at that hour to wake up the sleeping lion. Hearing the noise, Sugrīva also woke up. Seeing his elder brother rushing towards someone who appeared hostile by all accounts, Sugrīva came up to assist his elder brother in the face of emergency.

Māyāvī saw Bālī rushing towards him. He also noticed his younger brother following him. Fear overtook him. Terrorised, he ran away for safety. Bālī and Sugrīva chased him.

Having run a long distance, he (Māyāvī) came across a cave. Its wide mouth was covered with grass. The demon entered the cave and remained hidden for fifteen days. Bālī, desperate and mad in anger, commanded Sugrīva to wait at the mouth cautiously and entered the cave himself.

Bālī had asked Sugrīva to wait for him at the mouth of the cave for fifteen days. Sugrīva waited for him for one month with full precaution and alertness. He also tried to hear some sound coming from inside the cave. But he could hear only the noise of the demons. No signal came from Bālī. He got worried for his elder brother. Suddenly he saw a foaming stream of blood flowing out of the cave. Brotherly affection moved him inwardly. He got anxious for his brother. A doubt arose in his mind. Even very minute and carefull scanning on the part of Sugrīva could not lead him to the voice of Bālī. Then he thought his dear brother had been done away with by the demon. He also apprehended an attack on himself. In desperate frenzy of fear he studded the mouth of the cave with a rock, as big as a mount. Morose, Sugrīva, offered water in prayer for the deceased and returned home.

Sugrīva did not want to make the news of the death of his elder brother public. But the ministers, thinking that prince Angada was a minor, crowned Sugrīva. He began to perform the duties of the state in accordance with the laws of ethics.

Bālī, on the other hand, having finished Māyāvī and his lieutenants, returned to the capital. When he found Sugrīva enjoying the status of the king in his absence, he flared up in anger. He thought, "This selfish brother of mine with a design over my wife and kingdom, studded the mouth of the cave with a large rock so that I could not come out and might perish in the cave itself." This thought worked as the fat in the fire. Anger flared up further and further. Bālī lost all balance and reason in the frenzy of anger.

As soon as he saw his elder brother Bālī in a frenzy of anger, Sugrīva returned his kingdom to him. He tried to explain to him the real situation but in vain. Bālī became a dead enemy of Sugrīva. He brought the kingdom and Sugrīva's wife Rumā under his control. He designed to kill him even. Sugrīva alongwith the ministers escaped from the kingdom.

Terrified Sugrīva was heading for safety and Bali was pursuing him for his life. Sugrīva, while racing for safety, was leaving rivers, small and big, forests, mountains, oceans and towns behind. He had lost all his courage. He could not stay even for a couple of days anywhere because Bālī was chasing him for his life and like an enemy, was after his blood.

Sugrīva raced up to the Himālayas, the Meru and the north ocean but could not get refuge anywhere. Hanumāna was following his friend Sugrīva like a shadow. Suddenly the event of killing of the demon Dundubhi came to his mind. He apprised Sugrīva of the curse of the great sage Mataṅga. The curse was that if Bālī entered the hermitage of the sage Mataṅga, his head would split into hundreds of pieces. "Therefore that place would be safe for us", Hanumāna advised his master and friend Sugrīva. "Our stay in the hermitage on the mount would be safe, free of fear and comfortable", He said to Sugrīva.

Sugrīva on the advice of his dear secretary, Hanumāna jī went into the hermitage of the sage Mataṅga on the mount Ṛṣyamūka and lived there in peace. As Bālī, fearing the curse of the sage Mataṅga, could not go there, he returned home.

āsmin āšramamaṇḍale
pravišed yadi va bālī/murdhāsya šatadhā bhavet
[va. Rāmāyaṇa 4/46/22-23]

Well-read in state polity as he was, Bālī desired to retain Hanumāna jī, the son of the God of Wind, with himself honourably but he was the real friend of Sugrīva and his true well wisher. In the days of comfort and prosperity, many mean flatterers flock around the wealthy person but all abandon him in the days of distress and misery. The real friends and true servants do not deviate aside the way of love and dedication.

The son of Añjanā had lived with Sugrīva in happiness and wealth. How could he abandon him when he was in peril. He always moved with him, cared for his comfort and convenience, managed for his provision, always counselled when needed and consoled him in distress. His assurance was firm, and trust, unwavering. Sugrīva, therefore enjoyed his distress as happiness. He was not a secretary to Sugrīva but a true friend, loving companion and as good as the real brother.

Although deprived of everything and ousted from the place by Bālī, Sugrīva, on account of the association with Hanumāna jī, lived as a monarch on the mount Ṛṣyamūka with ease and in comfort.

Bālī could not find access to the mount Ṛṣyamūka because of the curse of the sage but he could depute some powerful fighter from his kingdom to finish him. Sugrīva was well aware of this possibility. But, he did not harbour any worry in his inner self as he had the firm faith in the power, valour, zeal and unique intelligence of Hanumāna jī, who was always prompt in service and compliance. Sugrīva always felt grateful to his destiny for its great gift in the form of Hanumāna jī as his secretary and companion.

At the Lotus Feet of His Lord

In compliance with the command of his father, Śrī Rāma, alongwith his loving and faithful wife Sītā, the daughter of Janaka jī, and younger brother Lakṣmaṇa, went into the forests. He roamed Citrakūṭa and Daṇḍakārṇya for thirteen years. During this period he obliged the sages and the great inspired personages. He finished the demons who troubled them and presented obstacles in the performance of their religious rites. Śrī Rāma made lives of the sages free of distress.

In the fourteenth year Rāma and Lakṣmaṇa constructed a hut of leaves and stalk, and began living therein. One day Rāvaṇa, the king of Laṅkā, came down to roam in front of the hut, in the guise of the golden deer. Sītā, the daughter of Janaka jī, noticing the unique animal, felt allured towards it. She entreated Rāma to catch and bring that deer. Śrī Rāma pursued the deer. The deceitful Rāvaṇa, seeing that Rāma was away, abducted Sītā, took her to Laṅkā and kept her in the Aśoka Vātikā, the grove of the Aśoka trees. Roaming in search for her, the daughter of Śrī Janaka jī, Rāma and Lakṣmaṇa reached the foothills of the mount of Ṛṣyamūka. In between they had finished the demons Viradha and Kabandha.

Sugrīva was always apprehensive of the designs of his elder brother, Bālī. When Sugriva was in a session with his ministers on a peak, he beheld the two brilliant brothers, gleaming like Gods, sporting bows and arrows, having large eyes and radiating aura around them; he trembled in apprehension.

Restless, he spoke to Hanumāna jī, "Beholding these two brave warriors, I am terror-stricken. It is possible, Bali has deputed them to finish me off. Kings have many friends.

Trusting them would be a folly. The clever man should try to identify the enemies moving in the disguise of a friend. Deceitful persons very successfully earn the favour and trust of others, but they themselves do not trust others. As soon as they get the opportunity, they assault them fiercely to finish them who come to trust them. Bālī is very clever in such things. Therefore, O great among the monkeys! You reach them as an ordinary person and ascertain their intentions. If you find that they have been commissioned by Bali to finish me off, you signal to me from there. Instantly I will leave this place and escape to safety, alongwith my ministers."

The son of the God of Wind had not been able to recognise his master by this time. Both brothers were sporting large bows and arrows. One of them was fair complexioned and the other not so fair. Still Śrī Hanumāna jī was not able to identify them. But his right side limbs were twitching and it was a good omen. His eyes brimmed with tears, and his heart throbbed with enchantment towards them.

Comprehending the intention of Sugrīva, Hanumāna jī started hopping down the mount. On the way he changed over to the guise of a brāhmana. Viewing the charms of Śrī Rāma and Śrī Lakṣmaṇa, as he had not seen or heard of before, Hanumāna jī entered into a unique state of mind. His forehead spontaneously bowed down at the feet of the Lord. Then, his hands folded in reverence, he enquired in a very polite and charming speech, "O, the brave and handsome warriors! Who are you? One of you is dark and the other fair. Certainly you are from one of the warrior clans. You are supreme among the brave. But you are nimble and soft. Here the mountains and forests are wild and frightful. All around roam the predators and other beasts. The ways are infested with overgrowing thorny bushes and grass. The pebbles on the paths pierce the foot soles. Certainly this land is not suitable for the feet of persons like you. Still, what is that which causes you to roam about in this forest where no human being dwells."

Hanumāna jī further implored, "I am amazed to see your brilliance. An ordinary young man from the warrior clan cannot be so brilliantly fiery as you both are. You possess the celestial splendour as is not to be found among the men of the earth. Who are you? Please, enlighten me as to whether you are Brahmā or Viṣnu or Maheṣa. Are you one of these or are you Nara or Nārāyana? Or, are you the Lord of the supreme consciousness itself, come down to the earth as a pair of the brave to alleviate the burden? Have you come down to oblige me and bless me with the realisation of the fulfilment?"

Hanumāna jī was a cultured person endowed with a unique skill in conversation. Having heard him speak, Śrī Rāma, addressing Lakṣmaṇa, said, "Brother! it is evident from his flawless articulation and erudite speech that he is well versed in the knowledge of grammar. He has studied the Vedas also. Certainly he has acquired a thorough knowledge of all the scriptures because he speaks a language which is unique, besides being ornate with the qualities called saṁskāra and karma and has an uninterrupted flow. His speech pleases the hearer deeply. It is endowed with the quality of auspiciousness. His speech manifests itself from three points, the heart, the throat and the head. Who will not feel gratified to hear such a speech?. Even the enemy, holding the sword high in the hand to kill him, having heard such a unique speech, as spoken by him, would change his heart, You, please, converse with him."

Having listened to the command of the elder brother, Lakṣmaṇa spoke to the son of the God of Wind who was in the guise of a brāhmana, "Brāhman! we are the sons of the king of Ayodhyā, Daśaratha, who enjoyed renown for the observance of piety. He is my elder brother, Śrī Rāma, I am Laksṃaṇa. By the order of our father we have come to stay in the forest for fourteen years. Here in the Pañcwatī, his wife was abducted by some deceitful demon. We are roaming in this dense forest only to look for her. Who are you?"

Hanumāna jī was getting acquainted with both of them but his attention was riveted on the countenance of Śrī Rāma. The matted locks of hair were enhancing the charm of the divine face, which was as lovely as a blossoming lotus. The hue of his body was as that of the rainy cloud. His eyes were gleaming a sense of kind benevolence. His body parts were flourishing with freshness and energy. The charm of his beauty was permeating into the entire being of Śrī Hanumāna jī. Having known who he was, he lost awareness of his self. The son of the God of Wind lay prostrate at the holy and divine feet of Śrī Rāma. They elevate and purify the soul. Their kind cannot be gotten in the three worlds. The sentiments of love and devotion arose like a tide in the heart of Śrī Hanumāna jī. It moved his soul deeply and fully. Restless and overwhelmed, he fell at his feet and a stream of tears, flowing out of his eyes, washed them. The feet of Śrī Rāma help the devotees cross the ocean of life and the world.

The flow of the tears of the son of Añjanā was not reaching the culminating state. His speech had choked. Managing himself somehow and with hands folded, he entreated thus.

"O, the embodiment of mercy! Me, the low, the base, could not recognise you, I forgot; this was natural. But how is it? You are acting as an ignorant person, and putting the question as this. How did you forget me? If not you, your lotus feet, the protector of the three worlds, who will protect me. O, the ocean of mercy, have compassion for me. O, the lord! accept me and make me your servant."

Certainly the lord is the embodiment of compassion. Out of the feet, emanates and swells the ocean of kindness to overwhelm the hearts of human beings. But he loves plain simplicity and detests concealment. The veil will obscure the vision. "He, who is the generous and the compassionate, expects and sees only the plain and simple heart and here, me, the son of the wind, was in the guise of a brāhmana, sporting a veil of falsehood over my real self. That is why, Śrī Rāma though viewing me with unblinking eyes, was keeping silent", contemplated Śrī Hanumāna.

Hanumāna jī was getting impatient. Crying his heart out, he implored, "Lord! I am stricken with ignorance, groping in darkness and crooked by heart, over that you have forgotten me. Where shall I seek refuge? You are compassion personified. Have compassion on me."

"Primarily, I am ignorant, possessed and gripped by attachment, crooked and mindless. Over that, my lord who is powerful, capable and the friend of the destitute, has ignored me."

Entreating heartily with a crying soul, Hanumāna jī lost awareness of his self. Inadvertently he also lost consciousness of his guise. Now in a real state of being, he was crying at the feet of his master and praying. Śrī Rāma beheld Hanumāna, his sincere devotee, in the true form of a monkey. As Rāma is compassion personified, instantly he lifted him up and hugged him fast to his bosom. At that time, the state of both the Lord and the devotee, was peculiar. Śrī Rāma was caressing the forehead of his devotee and the devotee, clinging to his large bosom, was sobbing as a baby. His voice had choked.

Assured of the affection of Śrī Rāma, Hanumana jī bowed his head at the feet of Lakṣmaṇa, the younger brother of Śrī Rāma. He too lifted him up and embraced him to his bosom. Later Hanumāna jī gave an account of the condition of Sugrīva. Eyes fixed at the countenance of Śrī Rāma, Hanumāna jī, who knew quite well how to conduct the negotiation, proceeded with the statement that on account of terrific enmity of his elder brother, Bālī, Sugrīva camps at Ṛsyamūka mountain. He is exiled from the kingdom and exceedingly suffering the separation from his wife. He is passing the days of suffering and woe in the midst of the forests and the mounts. You are also passing through a similar agony. Sugrīva needs the help and support of a capable power. He would feel immensely happy if you established a cordial friendship with him. And, having regained his kingdom and wife, he would render a valuable help and assistance in the search for and the recovery of Sīta jī. I therefore beseech you kindly to make friends with him.

As soon as Śrī Rāma nodded, he mounted both the brothers on his shoulders and started off for the Ṛsyamūka mountain. Seeing Hanumāna jī returning with Śrī Rāma and Lakṣmaṇa, Sugrīva felt assured and immensely happy.

Hanumāna jī, carrying Śrī Rāma and Lakṣmaṇa on his shoulders, reached the place of Sugrīva. He offered respect to both the brothers. Hanumāna introduced Sugrīva to Śrī Rāma. Then he produced fire with the help of a pair of flints. In the presence of the God, fire both promised to be friends and remain so in matters of distress, need and peril. This pleased both Śrī Rāma and Sugrīva. Then Śrī Rama, virtue personified, and Sugrīva, the chief of the monkey clan, sat side by side on the bed of leaves and flowers made by Hanumāna jī. He then offered a flowering branch of the sandal wood to Śrī Lakṣmaṇa to sit on.

Sugrīva in a very spirited manner, arousing sympathy and compassion in the heart of Śrī Rāma, related his tale of suffering and woe. He said, "O, scion of the lineage of Raghu! Bālī, my elder brother, having taken my dear wife away from me in a very cruel manner, exiled me from the kingdom. Terrified, I never get repose of mind. Agony of the separation from my wife and the torture of humiliation among my kith and kin, keep me awake at night. Please, make me free of the fear."

Śrī Rāma extended a promise of protection to him. He said, "My dear friend Sugrīva, I will finish Bālī off with a single arrow. Trust me. My arrow never goes futile. The life of Bālī will not be saved. Even the Gods will find it impossible to save him".

The single arrow of the Lord of the world, Śrī Rāma, the destroyer of the evil, killed Bālī, He left the sheath of the body in his presence. Hearing that her husband was no more alive, Tārā came there and wailed in sorrow. Hanumāna jī, who is supreme among those who have conquered passion, consoled her saying "Lady! A man performs the actions induced by the tendencies of virtue or vice. He reaps the evil or the good fruit of these actions in the next world. In fact you yourself deserve to be grieved for. For whom are you mourning? For him who deserved regrets? You are miserable and you feel pity for him who is now ruined. Human body is like a bubble. Living in this body, who should lament for whom? you are a learned lady, you know that transcience of the body, though certain, cannot be predicted. Therefore, only the virtuous deeds should be performed not the worldly and vile ones such as lamenting and crying".

Guṇadoṣkritam jantu, svakarmaphalahetukam,
Avyagrastadavāpnoti, sarvampretyašubhāshubham,
Šocyā šocasi kam šocyam, dīnaṁ dīnānukampase,
Kašca kasyānušocyosti, dehesmin budbudopame,
Jānāsyaniyaniyatāmevaṁ, bhātānāmagatim gatim
Tasmāchabham hikartavyam, panḍite nehu luukikam
[va. Rāmāyaṇa-4/21/2-3, 5]

गुणदो षक तम् जन्तुः स्वकर्मफलहेतुकम्
अव्यग्रस्तदवाप्नोति सर्व प्रेत्य शुभाशुभम्।
शोच्या शोचसि कम् शोच्यम् दीनम् दीनानुकम्पसे
कश्च कस्यानुशोच्यो स्तिदेहेस्मिन् बुदबुदोपमे
जानास्यनियता मेवं भूतानामँगतिं गतम्
तस्माच्छुभम् हि कर्तव्यम्, पण्डिते नेह लौकिकम्।
(रामायण 4/21/2-3,5)

He consoled her about Aṅgada,

"Your son Aṅgada is not yet adult. You should look after his good development. Think and plan for his accomplishments in future."

Aṅgadastu kumāroyaṁ draṣṭavyo jīvaputrayā,
Āyatyāṁca vidheyāni samarthanyasya cintaya
[va. Rāmāyana-4/21/4]

अड़्.दस्तुकुमारो यम्, द्रष्टव्यो जीवपुत्रया,
आयत्यांच विधेयानि समर्थान्य स्य चिन्तय।।

(रामायण 4/21/4)

Sugrīva ascended the throne of Kiṣkindhā with full ceremonial rites as prescribed in the scriptures. Aṅgada, the son of Bālī, was declared crown prince. Sugrīva regained wealth, kingdom and his wife—all that for which one aspires. Śrī Rāma is the defender of the defenseless. What remains beyond reach when he is to vouchsafe everything desired for?

Sugrīva began living in Kiṣkindhā. But Śrī Rāma did not enter the city. He honoured the command of his late father. He went to the mount Pravarṣaṇa to stay there for the rainy months.

Śrī Hanumāna yearned to remain in audience of Śrī Rāma for every moment of his life. But Sugrīva had just taken up the responsibility of the kingdom. A capable secretary was badly required to assist him in the discharge of the duties of the state. For this reason Śrī Rāma asked him to comply with the commands of Sugrīva. The command of Śrī Rāma was supreme for Hanumāna ji. He willingly opted to stay with Sugrīva in Kiṣkindhā.

Good Advice to Sugrīva

Śrī Rāma with Śrī Lakṣmaṇa was passing days at the mount Pravarṣaṇa, worrying enormously for his wife, Sīta. Sugrīva on the other hand lived in luxury. He was immensely happy to have gained wealth, kingdom and his wife Rumā. Besides, he had Tārā, the widow of his elder brother, Bālī. She was the spotless beauty personified. He indulged in gratifying pleasures unrestrained. He got absorbed in the indulgence to the extent that the consideration of the friendship with Śrī Rāma Candra, his favour and duty towards him on all these counts were completely out of his mind. But Hanumāna jī understood the real sense of the scriptures. He had the true knowledge of what is to be done and what not. As a secretary, he was ever alert, cautious, attentive and thoroughly apt in the art of conversation. The cause of Śrī Rāma remained constantly in his mind. He was all the time agitated by and engrossed in the worry to probe for and find the clues to the recovery of Sītā jī.

Hanumāna jī noted the change in season. The sky was clear. The waters in the rivers were no more muddy. The roads were dry and worthy of journeying. But, Sugrīva, the king of the monkeys, was careless in the matters of piety and the polity. Having obtained the desired objects, he was tending to act as he liked. One day Hanumāna jī went to

1. Rajyam Praptaīm yasgceiva kaulīšrīrabhivardhitā.	1. श्राज्यम् प्राप्तम् यशश्चैव कौली श्रीरभिवर्धिर्ता
2. Mitrāṇām saṅgraha: šeṣa stad bhavān kartamarhati	2. मित्राणाम् सड्.ग्रहः शेषस्तद् भवान कर्तुमर्हति।

3. Taddhavān vrittasampanna: sthita: pathi niratyaye	3. तद्भवान व त्तसम्पन्नः स्थितः पथि निरत्यये।
4. Mitrarthamabhinitārtham yathavat kartumarhati	4. मित्रार्थ ममिनीतार्थम् यथावत् कर्तुमर्हति।।
5. Tadidam mitrakaryam na: kālātitamrindam	5. तदिदम मित्र कार्यम् नः कालातीतम रिन्दम।
6. Kriyatām raghavasyeitad veidehya: parimārgaṇam	6. क्रियताम् राघवस्यैतद वैदेह्याः परिमार्गणम
7. Naca kālam atītaṁ te nivedayati kālavit	7. नच कालमतीतम ते निवेदयति कालवित्।
8. Tvaramaṇopi sa prajña: tava rājan vaša̅nuga:	8. त्वरमणो पि सप्राज्ञः तव राजन् वशानुग।
9. Na hi tāvad bhavet kalo vyatītaščodanadṛte	9. नहि तावत् भवेत् कालो व्यतीत श्चोदना दते।
10. Coditasya hi kāryasya bhaveit kāla vyatikrma:	10. चेदितस्य हि कार्यस्य भवेत काल व्यतिक्रम।
11. Shakti manotivikānto vanrarkshaganeshwera	11. शक्तिमानतिविक्रान्तो वानरर्क्षगणेश्वर।
12. Kartum dāšarathe: arati magyam kimnu sajjase	12. कर्तुम दाशरथेः प्रीति माज्ञायाम किंनु सज्जसे।।
13. Prāṇatyagavišakena kṛtam tena mahat priyam	13. प्राण त्यागाविशङ्केन क तम तेन महत् प्रियम्
14. tasya mārgama veidehīm prithivyāmapi cāmbare	14. तस्य मार्गाम वैदेहीम् प थिव्यामपि चाम्बरे।।

15. dēva dānava gandharvā asurā samrudgaṇa:	15. देव दानव गन्धर्वा असुराः समरूद्गणा।
16. Na cha yaksa: bhayam tasya kuryu: kimiva rākshasā:	16. न च यक्षा भयं तस्य कुर्युः किमिव राक्षसा।
17. tadevaṁ šaktiyukt asya nūrvaṁ nratikṛtastatha	17. त्वदेव शक्तियुक्तस्य पूर्वम् प्रतिक तस्तथा।
18. Rāmasyarhasi pingeša kartum sarvātmanā priyam. [va.Rama 4/29]	18. रामास्यार्हसि पिङ्गेशं कर्तुम् सर्वात्मना प्रियम्। (वा. रा. 4/29, 9,12,15,16,21,23,25)

him and gave him an advice which was truthful, agreeable and propitious.

"Master! you have obtained the kingdom; you have earned fame also. The wealth in the treasury has swelled. The object of winning over friends remains to be accomplished. It should be achieved now in time. You are endowed with virtues and tread the path of piety. Therefore, the promise to carry out, that you have given out to your friend, should be properly kept. You have the calibre to crush the enemy, Śrī Rāma is our real and close friend. The time for his mission is running out. We should embark on the plan to find Sītā as early as possible. Still he depends on you. He is hesitating to press for urgency. He is waiting patiently and does not say that the time was running out. If we embark upon the mission before he comes out with the reminder, time will not he considered as out. If he comes and urges for assistance, it will be taken as our negligence and indifference and that we have idled away time. You are the lord of the clans of the monkeys and the bears. You are gifted with the zeal also. Why are you then defering to order them into action. Śrī Rāma did not think twice to take the life of Bālī. He has accomplished a very great and very important task for you.

Now it is incumbent upon you that we go and spread out in search for his spouse on the earth and in the sky. The Gods, the demons, the gandharvas, the asuras, the winds and the yakṣas even cannot terrify him away off the line of his action, what to say of the rākṣās. The lord of the monkeys! the mission of such a personage as Rāma, the all powerful, should be kept as the top priority. He has already done a great favour to you. The reciprocal response from our end is highly expected. We should do it with all our might."

The venerable and the wise king of the monkeys dreaded the delay in the action for Śrī Rāma. He always respected the advice of Hanumāna. Pleased at the homely advice from him to embark upon the plan for the search, he instantly ordered the brave monkey, Nīla, to gather and present all the enterprising, fast moving group leaders and brave soldiers, in his audience within fifteen days. Urgings for the imminence of action, he declared that the person reaching after the date shall be liable to lose his life.

On the other hand Śrī Rāma, thinking Sugrīva to be inactive and careless, even on setting in of the autumn after the rainy season, lost his patience. He said to Lakṣmaṇa, "Sugrīva had fixed the time for the search of Sītā, but now after his selfish objective was met, the silly monkey is ignoring me."

"He thinks that I am an exiled, fatherless and helpless person and I seek refuge under him. Brother Lakṣmaṇa ! go and tell him that person is the vilest in the world who having promised to help a man of power, calibre and zeal, longing for some hope to be fulfilled, goes back on his word of promise after his objectives are met as a result of the acts which the powerful man did to favour him. That person is the greatest, and the bravest who, having spoken the word of promise, good or otherwise, keeps it for the sake of truth. Such persons hold that the promise must be kept in every way."

Śrī Rāma with agony in his heart, further said to his younger brother, "Go and tell that wicked monkey that the path by which Bālī has been dispatched has not yet been closed. I had finished Bālī alone at that time. This time if he does not keep his word of honour, I will dispatch him along with his kith and kin to the other world."

The words of Śrī Rāma flared up the flame of anger in the heart of Śrī Lakṣmaṇa. He lay prostrate at the feet of his elder brother and submitted, "That stupid monkey, in the presence of the fire God as a witness, had established friendship. But now when his objectives are met his intentions have changed. Right now I will kill that faithless Sugrīva and will crown prince Aṅgada as the monarch of the Kiṣkindhā state. Now, he, Aṅgada, with the help and the assistance of the monkey warriors will find the clues to the place where Sītā has been kept in concealment."

Seeing Lakṣmaṇa flaring up and setting out with bow and arrow to kill Sugrīva, Śrī Rāma, who is infinite patience personified, the embodiment of the rules of morality, the soul of the universe incarnate, counselled him saying, "Lakṣmaṇa! a strong man like you should not do the forbidden act of killing a friend. He, who is able to restrain his anger with the help of right judgments, is the best among the men. Dear, he is my friend. You please do not kill him. You only frighten him saying that he will be killed as was Bālī. You return soon with his response."

Lakṣmaṇa, the son of Sumitrā, the lion among the descendents of Ikṣvāku, bowed his head at the feet of Śrī Rāma and proceeded saying, "As you command." At that time, on account of the flaring anger, his countenance was looking extremely terrible. His lower lip was twitching. He was breaking and felling the shrubs and plants in the way. He was throwing the peaks of the mounts away. He was looking Rudra, the fierce destroyer. On reaching the vicinity of Kiṣkindhā, he pulled the string of his bow and sent out the terrible reverberating sound all around. Some ordinary monkeys on the fortification wall of the town carrying stones and branches of trees in their hands, began to raise sounds. This added fuel to the flaring fire of the anger of Lakṣmaṇa. He placed a terrible arrow on his bow and had hardly pulled it to destroy the town Kiṣkindhā when the whole army of brave monkeys trembled in fear.

Seeing the populace disturbed, crown prince Aṅgada came forward to Lakṣmaṇa and bowed his head in reverence to him. Instantly his anger calmed. Keeping him close to his chest, he bade him, "Dear Aṅgada! you at once go to Sugrīva and tell him that Śrī Rāma is extremely angry with him. On his bidding I have come here."

"All right", Aṅgada said politely and taking his leave with his folded hands, went to Sugrīva. As soon as he came to know about the anger of Śrī Rāma, fear overtook him. Soon he dispatched Hanumāna jī to pacify Lakṣmaṇa.

Hanumāna jī came down to Lakṣmaṇa, touched his feet in devotion and entreated him saying:

एहि वीर महाभाग भवद्गृहमशंकितम् ।।
प्रविश्य राजदारादीन्, दष्ट्वा सुग्रीवमेव च।
यदाज्ञापयसे पश्चात् तत् सर्वं करवाणि भोः ।।

(आध्यात्म रामायणम्–४/५/३७–३८)

ehi vīra mahābhāga bhavadgriham šaṅkitam,
pravisyarājdārādīn dristvā sugrīvameva ca,
yadagyapaya se paścāttat sarvam karavāṇi bhoṛ.

(आध्यात्म रामायणम्–४/५/३७–३८)

"O highly distinguished soul! This is your own mansion, enter it freely. Meet king sugrīva and his dames. I will comply with all your commands."

Hanumāna jī, the son of the God of Wind, held the hands of Lakṣmaṇa, the younger brother of Śrī Rāma, in great esteem and conducted him through the town to the regal palace. Here Tārā, the honey tongued lady, welcomed Lakṣmaṇa and apprised him of the worry of Sugrīva. She said, "Sugrīva is very much worried because of the mission of Śrī Rāma. Please, come in the king's palace and extend to him security of fearlessness."

In the palace Sugrīva and his wife Rumā offered their obeisance at the feet of Lakṣmaṇa. There too Hanumāna jī, endowed with political wisdom, spoke to him:

"O great master! this king of the monkeys is given to the cause of Śrī Rāma with dedication. For the sake of Rāma's mission, he keeps awake at night; O capable! see that multitudes of the monkeys are flocking in from all quarters; soon they all will leave in the search for Sītā. King Sugrīva will carry out the mission of Śrī Rāma jī to success."

After that, Sugrīva bowed at the feet of Lakṣmaṇa jī and spoke to him in a very polite manner, "Lord! I am the slave of Śrī Rāma Candra. He alone saved my life. This wealth, this prosperity and this kingdom all are mine today as a blessing of Śrī Rāma. He is capable of vanquishing the warriors of the three worlds. In his mission I will merely be an instrument. I am the vile, the mean, the beast engrossed in the pursuit of the sensual gratification only. I am yours in every way. Please pardon me for my failings."

Hearing the prayer of Sugrīva, the son of Sumitrā held him by the arm and clung him to his bosom affectionately. Addressing him, he said, "O distinguished soul! Please do not take to your heart what I said to you earlier. It was an expression of anger in love. Śrī Rāma is living singly in the forests and is deeply feeling the agony of separation from Sītā. We should go to him without delay."

"Yes we should move to him at once", said Sugrīva. He washed the feet and hands of Lakṣmaṇa in devotion, offered him flowers in admiration and mounted the regal chariot with him. They proceeded for the place where Śrī Rāma was dwelling. The distinguished among the monkeys, Aṅgada, Naīl and the Hanumāna proceeded to meet Śrī Rāma Candra. At that time various percussion instruments were played in a procession.

Setting Out in Search for Sītā

Śrī Rāma was sitting on a deer-skin on a boulder at the mouth of a cave and watching the flocks of birds in a melancholy mood. The matted locks of hair were adorning his face and the head as a crown. His body was of the complexion of the clouds of the rainy season. As soon as Sugrīva and Lakṣmaṇa had glimpses of Śrī Rāma from a distance, they at once alighted from the chariot. Śrī Rāma's countenance showed his inner peace. Sugrīva ran towards Śrī Rāma and, like an innocent child, fell at his lotus feet and began crying. Śrī Rāma, who is compassion personified, at once lifted him up and clasped him to his bosom. He offered him a seat and enquired about his family welfare.

Sugrīva folded his hands and submitted in utter politeness, "Lord! I am not at fault. Your illusory supernatural power is very pervasive. Only with your favour and devotion this can be overcome. I am a vile beast given to the pursuit of sensual gratification alone. Have mercy on me, Lord Have compassion on me."

Śrī Rāma, compassion incarnate, patted his head. At the same time, a multitude of monkey fighters could be seen approaching.

Seeing them Sugrīva submitted to Śrī Rāma, "Lord! All these troops of the monkeys and the sleuths of bears are your obedient servants. They live only by fruits and roots. This Jambvān is the leader of the bears. He is a very powerful and dexterous fighter and extremely wise. He is the leader of ten million fighters and the foremost among my ministers. The bear soldiers under him are very obedient, disciplined and live only on vegetarian diet. Besides, Nala, Nīla, Gavaya,

Gavakṣa, Gandhamādana, Śarabha, Mainda, Gaja, Panasa, Balīmukha, Dadhimukha, Suṣeṇa, Tāra and the father of Hanumāna, Śrī Kesarī, are commanders of my army. Among them Kesarī is very brave and resolute. He is the commander-in-chief of my forces. Under him are the monkey warriors who command as enormous size as that of the mounts. Their valour is of the extreme degree."

"All these will sacrifice their lives for you in the battles and will feel happy to have done so. Please, command them as you will."

Śrī Raghunātha jī, the embodiment of all the powers, spoke to Sugrīva:

"Sugrīva! you know your mission. If you think it proper, please, command them to search for Sītā."

Sugrīva, thus commanding the army leaders to go out carefully in search for Sītā, said, "Complying with my commands, you all go out and return within one month. If you spend a day over a month and are not able to find her, O monkeys, you will receive the punishment of life at my hands."

Thus Sugrīva gave the strictest commands to the leaders of the troops of monkeys and sleuths of bears for the search for Sītā in a short time. He sent out the monkey soldiers in all directions. But he assigned the southern quarter to the mighty crown-prince, Aṅgada, Jāmbavān, Hanumāna, Nala, Suṣeṇa, Śarabha, Mainda and Dvivida, among others. At that time, commending Hanumāna he said:

"O, the best among the monkeys! I never see your movement and speed impeded on the earth, in the intermediate space between the earth and the heaven, the regions of the Gods or in waters. You command the knowledge of all the regions of the asuras, the gandharvas, the nāgas, the humans, the Gods and the regions covered by the oceans and the mountains. O, great and the brave monkey! You embody the unhindered movement everywhere, the speed, the brilliance, the ability to rebound and to spring – all qualities of your progenitor, the God of the Wind. There is none in this world who can equal you in brilliance. Therefore, how Sītā jī can be found out? You think about the means and the ways. You are the master of the scriptures relating to morality and conduct. You alone in this creation are the embodiment of power, might, intelligence, zeal, endeavour, adaptability to the needs of the time and space and behaviour in consonance with the laws of morality – all together."

Having conferred all praise on Hanumāna, Sugrīva bade adieu to the monkeys and the bears and ordered them again to find Sītā out. Then brave and mighty monkeys and bears came down to touch the feet for Śrī Rāma, received his blessings and went away on the mission. Last of all came the son of the God of Wind. Then Śrī Rāma conferred commendation on him saying, "O great among the brave, your endeavour, the patience and the zeal and the message of Sugrīva—all show that my mission will be fulfilled on account of your effort. You take this ring of mine. The syllables of my name are engraved on it. This is for your introduction. You give it to Sītā in a solitary situation. O the best among the monkeys! You alone are capable of discharging this duty. I very well know the might of your intelligence. Well, now take leave and proceed."

Hanumāna held the ring with due respect and kept it secured on his person. He bowed his head at the feet of Śrī Rāma. Śrī Rāma loves his devotees affectionately. His hand spontaneously went on to his forehead. With great difficulty he rose up, smeared his forehead with the sacred dust of his feet, enshrined his figure in his heart and set out courageously. The name of his lord was on his tongue which he was repeating incessantly.

A Devotee of Śrī Rāma

Hanumāna alongwith the monkey retinue in search for Sītā reached the dense forest in the ranges of Vindhya mountains. There the forests abounded in the thorny bushes and the dead woods. There was no trace of water. The troops of monkeys and the sleuths of bears, on account of enormous roaming, were getting restless for water. But water was not visible anywhere and due to excessive thirst, the palates and the gullets were getting dry. They had their hope only on Hanumāna who was with them. He looked around patiently. He sighted a giant cave at some distance. Its mouth was covered with grass, shrubs and creepers. He visualised swans, the curlew birds (a long billed bird), cranes and the cakra birds flying out of it, their wings and feathers were drenched in water. Inferring that water must be there, he asked them all to come there. Hanumāna was believed to have the knowledge of the impenetrable forests, and he was with them. Therefore, having faith in him, the troops of monkeys and sleuths of bears, holding hands of one another, proceeded to enter the cave cautiously. There was utter darkness upto some distance. After that they saw a lake of fresh water. On its rim were the trees like the sala (the Vatica Robusta), the tamala (the black Khadia), the Tala, the fan palm, the Barassees (Flabelliformis), the Nāgakesara (the michelia Champaka) and the Kanera (the Pteroshermum acerifolium). There were other trees flowering and laden with fruit also. Besides they came across a grand and splendid mansion, decorated with cloth and ornaments. There were heaps of eatables. Besides, they saw a very charming lady seated on a gold throne and donning the attire of bark and black deer skin. She was meditating at that time. Viewing her, they looked into one another's eyes. The body of meditating lady was emitting a peculiar radiance around it. The monkeys and the bears were overawed at it and they lay prostrate before her. The highly distinguished lady, viewing them in the venerating posture, spoke to them very calmly and in a very soft tone, "Who are you and for what purpose are you roaming these impenetrable forests? Why are you destroying the garden and the orchard?"

Hanumāna, the huge sized, responding very politely said, "Śrī Rāma, the son of the king Daśaratha of Ayodhyā, complying with his commands, had come to the forests accompanied by his younger brother, Lakṣmaṇa, and wife, Sītā. From there Rāvaṇa abducted his very faithful and docile wife, Sītā. On account of being his friend, Sugrīva deputed us to accomplish the mission of finding her out. We came here in pursuit of the same mission. We entered this cave looking for water and eatables because we all were extremely thirsty and hungry. Venerable lady! We are eager to know all about you. Please, enlighten us about yourself."

"My great fortune!" exclaimed the lady whose personality has been rendered pure and sacred by the constant pursuit of austere penance, fasting and strict observance of yoga practice. She gave out, "all my austerities and practices have yielded the auspicious result today. I feel fulfilled. I am enjoying infinite ecstasy today."

"You feel freely assured and harbour no worry in your mind. Pacify them if they are agitated on any account. You eat the nectar-like fruit to your full satiety and quench your thirst with fresh and cool water of the lake to your full satisfaction. Satisfied fully, you come to me, sit beside me and I will relate to you my story and tell you all about myself."

Hanumāna jī and his fellow monkeys ate the fruits and drank water. They were pleased with this sojourn in their indefinite pursuit. Then they came closer to the lady and sat down with docility to listen to her story.

"In the days bygone, there was a very beautiful daughter to Viśvakarmā. Her name was Hemā. Pleased at her unique dance, Lord Śiva easy to propitiate, vouchsafed this grand celestial town to her to live in."

"She lived here for a thousand years. She was my intimate friend and was dearer to me than my own self."

"A devotee of Lord Viṣṇu, she sincerely aspired for deliverance. So, when departing for the region of Brahman, she counselled me to propitiate Lord Viṣṇu in solitude, practising austerity and penance."

"Viṣṇu will be born to Kauśalyā, the fortunate wife of Daśaratha, as a son to her. In order to establish the rule of piety and virtue and to destroy the evil forces on the land, he will roam the forest. Searching for his supremely virtuous wife, some monkeys will come to you in this cave. You should welcome them with eatables and fresh drinking water," she had advised me then.

"Having treated them thus you should return to the regions of Śrī Rāma. Having had his glimpse, which even the great yogis yearn to have, you pray to him. By the grace of Śrī Rāma, you will enter into the blissful Samadhi in the eternal regions of Śrī Viṣṇu," she had apprised me of this future event in the bygone times.

The lady felt greatly obliged. Viewing Hanumāna jī with gratitude and affection, she further stated, "I am the daughter of the gandharva whose name is Divya. My name is Svayamprabha. I feel obliged by the events that have taken place today. The Sun of my luck has shone up today, as you all have put your holy feet here on this land. Now I am getting impatient to have the vision of my beloved deity Śrī Rāma." You close your eyes. Instantly you will reach out of this cave. You will get the clues to the place of Sītā. Do not lose heart", she concluded and blessed the monkeys and bears.

Following the dictate of the lady, the grand army of the monkeys and bears closed their eyes and instantly reached outside the forest.

Clue from Sampāti

The monkeys and the bears again engaged themselves in the search. In spite of the great effort, Sītā jī could not be traced. Fatigued and exhausted, monkeys and bears began exchanging views and opinions about the whole exercise. Extremely depressed, Aṅgada said, "We do not know what to do and where to go. For the last one month we have been roaming around this cave. The time limit allowed by king Sugrīva is about to be over. The whereabouts of the virtuous lady, Sītā, are not yet known. Now on returning to Kiṣkindhā, we all would be done to death. Above all and everybody, I will not be spared as I am the son of his enemy. I have been saved by the Lord Rāma, compassion and piety personified. On the pretext of not having found out Sītā, he will get me executed. How can he leave me? I will stay back and leave my body here."

Seeing the crown-prince crying, the monkeys and bears got extremely unhappy. With full and sincere sympathy, they spoke to Aṅgada, "Please, do not worry. We will sacrifice even our lives to save you. We will stay here in this cave which provides and offers heavenly comforts and luxuries to us." Monkeys had spoken these words in a hush hush manner, Somehow they reached the ears of Śrī Hanumāna jī. In full sympathy with him he said, "Prince! you are worrying for no reason. Is there any reason for such a worry? You being the dear son of queen Tārā, you are naturally dear to Sugrīva also. And love for you in the heart of Śrī Rāma is increasing day by day. You are dearer to him than Lakṣmaṇa is, the advice which these monkeys have rendered to you in favour of staying in this cave itself for a danger free living is useless, because no object in the three worlds is out of the mark and reach and impenetrable for his arrow. These monkeys have never suffered separation from their families. They are not aware of the agony of separation. So, their advice holds no good for you, Aṅgada."

Trying to make his point clear, he said, "Besides this, my dear, I place before you one secret. Listen carefully, Śrī Rāma is not an ordinary human being. He is the immutable, Lord Nārāyana Himself. Sītā jī none other than His illusory power. She keeps the creation in the state of enchantment. Lakṣmaṇa embodies in himself the power that supports and sustains the creation. He is truly the supreme serpent. Sīta jī provides the support to the three worlds. All these are born as human beings to carry out the mission of destroying the devilish forces on the earth on the request from Brahma jī, the creator. Anyone of these is capable of protecting the three worlds. Ours is the great fortune that we are associated with the mission and the playful acts of these mighty forces, as their instruments." Thus Hanuman jī consoled the crown Prince Aṅgada.

Hanumāna jī is endowed with the capability of showing the greatest power, might, courage and zeal. He alongwith Jāmbavān and other monkey and bear warriors, moving slowly in search of Sītā jī arrived at the shore of the southern sea. Behind them was the sacred valley of the Mahendra mountain and in front of them was the unfathomable boundless sea. The time limit of one month as allowed by their king Sugrīva for the search of Sītā jī had come to an end. Seeing the terrifying high waves of the boundless unfathomable sea in front of them, the monkey and the bear soldiers were overwhelmed with fear. Their wits were at a loss to comprehend the situation. They failed to understand what to do and where to go. Imagining the strict punishment that might fall on them from their king Sugrīva, they said, "The king was capable of meting out the strictest punishment even for a minute mistake or offence. He will certainly do away with us. It is better to embrace death by way of abstaining from food and water than to die at his hands. With this thought in their mind, they all sat down there on the mats of Kuša̅ grass.

Hearing the noise made by the monkeys and bears the vulture, Sampāti, came out of its cave. When he came to know that the monkeys and the bears were sitting there determined to forego water and food till they all had died, he felt exceedingly happy thinking that there would be no more scarcity of food. In wild excitement, Sampāti exclaimed:

Vidhih Kila naram loke vidhānenānuvartate!
Yathāyam vihito bhakṣyascirānmahyamupāgatah
Paramparāṇām bhakṣiṣye vānaraṇām mṛtaṁ mṛtam.

विधिः किल नंर लोके विधानेनानुवंर्तते
यथायम् विहितो भक्ष्यश्चिरान्महयमुपागतः
परम्पराणाम् भाक्षिष्ये वानराणाम् म तम म तम् ।
(वा. रा. ४/५६/४–५)

"The destiny moves the people according to their acts. As they sow so they reap. See, today enormous food has been made available to me after a long time. I will consume the monkeys one after another as they die out of starvation and thirst."

Seeing the huge vulture lolling its tongue, the monkeys and the bears got terrified. They thought neither they did any service to Śrī Rāma nor they complied with the command of their king Sugrīva. For no reason they find their way to the stomach of this vulture. Then within hearing of the huge vulture, who had no wings to fly, they spoke:

ahojāṭāyurdharmātma Rāmasyārthe mṛtaḥ sudhih!
mokṣam prāpa durāvāpaṁ yogināmapyarindamah !!

अहो जटायुधर्मात्मा रामस्यार्थे म तः सुधीः ।
मोक्षम् प्राप दुरावापम् योगिनामप्यरिन्दमः ।।
(अ.रा. ४/७/३४)

"How fortunate was Jaṭāyu, the pious, who lost his life in the service of Śrī Rāma. Thus he attained the deliverance which is difficult to attain even for yogins. Not only that, he died fighting the enemy of Śrī Rāma."

Hearing the name of Jaṭāyu, Sampāti became very sad. Surprised at the mention of the name, Jaṭāyu, he enquired of the monkeys:

केवायूयंम् मम भ्रातुः कर्णपीयूषसंनिभम् ।।
जटायुरिति नामाद्य व्याहरन्तः परस्परम् ।
उच्यताम् वो भयम् मा भून्मन्तः प्लवगसत्तमाः ।।
(अ.रा. ४/७/३५–३६)

ke vā yūyam mamabhrātuh: karṇapīyūsa samnibham
Jatāyuriti nāmādya vyāharantaḥ parasparam
ucyatamṁvo bhayam mā bhūnmattaḥ plavagasattamāh
[a. ram. 4/7/35-3]

"Good monkeys! Who are you? You mentioned among yourself the name Jaṭāyu. This name is very dear to me. It sounds very sweet for my ears, as sweet as nectar. Let there be no fear from me. Tell me all about yourself."

Inspite of the assurance accorded by Sampāti the leaders of the monkey troops did not trust him. They had all suspicion about the carnivorous vulture. After a long deliberation among themselves, the monkeys moved closer to him. Aṅgada, then, related the story of Śrī Rāma from his birth to the abduction of Sītā in full detail. After this he informed him of how fighting Rāvaṇa for Sītā he fell wounded and breathed his last in the lap of Śrī Rāma. He narrated his last rites as he, Śrī Rāma, had performed with full sentiment and elaboration. Lastly he said to him, "We monkeys have come up so far in seach for Sītā. Our king Sugrīva has commanded us for this mission. But no trace of her has been found till now. For this reason we grieve."

Sampāti felt ecstatic on having been apprised in full detail of the complete dedication of life for the cause for Śrī Rāma on the part of his dear brother, Jaṭāyu and then his last rites, culminating in the final deliverance of his soul. Not only this, he recalled the words of the God • oon and intuited that the last moment of his final emancipation had arrived. He forgot all his grief. The thrill and excitement of extreme happiness ran through his being:

अङ्.गदस्य वचः श्रुत्वा सम्पातिर्हृष्टमानसः ।।
उवाच मत्प्रियो भ्राता जटायुः प्लवगेश्वराः ।
बहुवर्षसहस्रान्ते भ्रात वार्ता श्रुता मया ।।
(अधया. रामाः ४/७/४६–४७)

Aṅgadasya vacaḥ šrutvā sampātirhṛṣṭamānasaḥ
Uvāca matpriyo bhrātā Jaṭāyuḥ plavageśvarḥ
Bahuvarṣasahasrānte bhrātṛvārta šruta mayā
(adhya. Rama 4/7/46-47)

Hearing the words of Aṅgada, Sampāti felt ecstatic. Addressing himself to the leaders of the monkeys, he said, "Jaṭāyu was my dear brother. Some news about him has reached my ears after the lapse of a thousand years."

"By all means I will perform, by my words and by my deeds, that which will do you all good and which you all will like. This is my firm belief that the service to Śrī Rāma is the duty of my life. There is no doubt about it."

"Take me to the shore of water. I will offer water from my palms to the soul of my deceased brother. Then I will show you the way to the success of your mission on which you have been sent."

Honouring the desire of Sampāti, Hanumāna jī lifted him up and took him to the shore of the sea. There Sampāti took bath. Then he offered water from his hollowed palms to the soul of his deceased brother for peace.

Monkeys then brought him back to his place. There he sat among the devotees of Śrī Rāma. Finding himself in front of and among the servants of Śrī Rāma he felt extremely happy. Agony of his mind and suffering of his body had already vanished. He cast his sight around and respectfully addressed the devotees, whom Śrī Rāma loved:

Giri Trikūṭa ūpara basa Laṅkā/taharaha rāvaṇa sahaja asaṁkā
Tahan asoka upabana jaha rahai / Sītā beiṭhi soca rata ahai
Mai dekhaū tumha nāhin / gīdhahidrsṭi apāra
Būrha bhayuna ta karateun / kachuka sahāya tumhār
[mānasa 4/27/6.28]

"Lanka is situated on the mount Trikūta. There lives Rāvaṇa without fear. There is a garden called Aśoka Vātikā. Therein stays Sītā enduring the agony of separation. I am seeing all but you cannot see all that. Vultures are endowed with limitless sighting faculty. I have grown very old. Otherwise I would have joined you in your mission."

Inspiring them further, he said,

"You all are gifted with keen intelligence, you are also powerful, wise and difficult to defeat even by Gods."

Tadbhavanto matiśreṣṭha / balavanto manasvinaḥ
Prahitaḥ kapirājena / deveirapi durāsadaḥ
[vā. Rāma. 4/59/25-26].

Later, commending the sharp arrows of Śrī Rāma and Lakṣmaṇa, he spoke to the monkeys and the bears assembled there:

Rāma Lakṣamaṇa āṇāśca vihitaḥ kankapatriṇaḥ
trayāṇāmapiokānam paryāptāstraṇanigrahe
kamam khalu dašgrīvastejobalasamanvitaḥ
bhavatām to samarthānām na kiňcidapi duṣkaram
[vā. Rāma. 4/59/26-27]

"The arrows for Śrī Rāma and Lakṣmaṇa have been made by the creator himself; they are fitted with the wings of the heron. They have power to protect and contain the three worlds. Daśagrīva, who holds ten heads on his shoulders, may command might and brilliance to his desire, but you are capable and nothing is difficult for you to achieve."

Having spoken the words of inspiration, he advised, "You try to cross the sea in some way or the other. Rāma himself will finish Rāvaṇa. You confer among yourselves and decide who from amongst you is the brave who can reach Laṅkā on the other shore of the sea and having seen and spoken to the mother Sītā, can return to this shore."

Having known the whereabouts of Sītā jī from Sampāti the monkeys and the bears felt very happy. Their joy was boundless. They felt curious about his life story also.

Sampāti narrated the events that had led to the burning of his wings. He also made the prophecy by Muni Candramā, known to them. He further said, "Dear monkeys and bears! What can be said of the bird whose wings are burnt? In this pitiable condition, which has befallen me, my son, Supārśva, alone has been arranging for my sustenance. Our appetite is always very pressing and unsatiable. One day I was getting very restless due to hunger; my son returned late that too empty handed. On this I admonished him and said many things which I ought not to have. On his part, he very politely said to me, 'In search of food for you I flew into the sky at the proper time. Having closed the door of mount Mahendra with my beak lowered, I was looking for food in the sea. At that time I visualized a mighty man forcibly carrying a very brilliant lady. I tried to satiate my hunger on them. He very politely entreated me not to hurt him or her. I came under the influence of the speech of that person. I left him.' Thus spoke my son to me".

"My son continued, 'Later, from the accounts given by the sages and accomplished saints I came to know that the lady of the celestial beauty and brilliance was Sītā, the wife of Śrī Rāma, the son of the king Daśaratha, and the black person who was carrying her was Rāvaṇa, the king of Laṅkā. The hair of Sītā was unkempt. In great anguish and agony, she was lamenting for Rāma and Lakṣmaṇa. She was dropping her ornaments also. For this reason my arrival was delayed.' concluded my son."

Having narrated the above episode Sampāti further spoke to the gathering of the monkeys and bears thus:

"Wingless, helpless and powerless, I only languished. I could do nothing but this. I was aware of the might of Rāvaṇa. I only scolded my son for having done nothing to save Sītā from Rāvaṇa." 'Sampāti expressed himself.

He further went on:

Tasyā vilapitāṃ šrutvā, tau ca Sītā viyojitau
Na me Daśrathasnehāt putreṇopāditam priyam
[va. Ra. 4/63/7-8]

"He heard the wails of Sītā, he knew that those two, Rāma and Lakṣmaṇa, were separated from her; he was not unaware of my affectionate relation with Daśaratha. Still, he did not protect Sītā jī. This did not please me. I only admonished him."

The most fortunate Sampāti, while narrating his life story to the monkeys and bears, discovered that two new wings had come out on his body. The power and might that usually go with young age, too erupted in him.

Recalling the words of the • oon, he rejoiced immensely. He told the monkeys:

sarvathā kriyatāṁ yatnaḥ Sitāmdhigamiṣyatha
pakṣalābho mamāyaṁ vaṛ siddhipratyayakārakaḥ

"Certainly you will meet Sītā. The fact that I have regained my wings points to the certainty that you will succeed in your mission."

Then he elaborated upon the auspicious powers of the name of Śrī Rāma. He said that the task of crossing the sea is easy for Rāma. Sampāti expressed his sentiment thus :

yannāmasmṛtimātrato parimitaṁ saṁsāravārāṁnidhim
tīrtvā gachati durjanopi paramam višnoḥ padam šašvatam
tasyeiva sthitikāriṇastrijagatām Rāmasya bhaktaḥ priyā
yūyam kim na samudramātra taraṇe śaktaḥ katham vānarā
[A. Rāmā/8/55]

"My dear monkeys and bears!

The name of Śrī Rāma has all the powers. Even the devilish souls, merely meditating on it, transcend the apparently boundless ocean of the worldness onto the region of Viṣṇu. You are his dear devotees, Why and how will you not be able to cross this negligible and narrow strip of water?"

The docile, powerful, mightily courageous and ardent Hanumāna, the son of the God of Wind, was listening to each and every word of Sampāti attentively. On having known the exact and clear account of the place of Sītā Hanumāna's joy reached a state of ecstasy. The thrill of joy ran through his being.

At this very time the great bird, Sampati, the vulture, flew away from the mount.

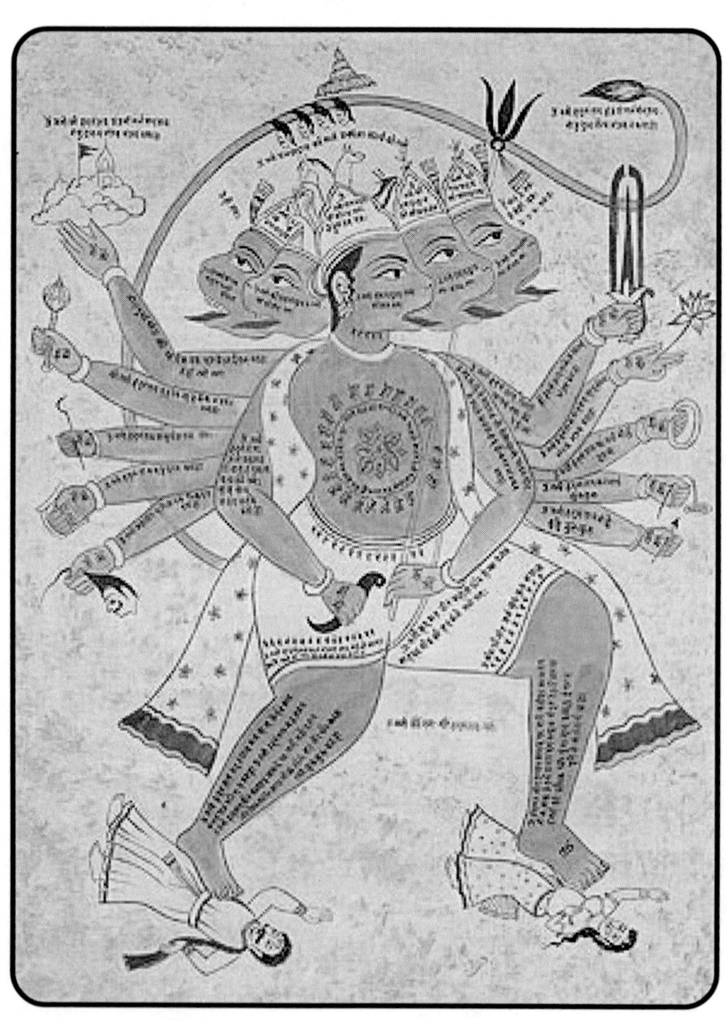

Crossing the Sea

Saṁpāti, the king of the vultures, told the monkeys and the bears where Sītā was kept by Rāvaṇa. The wave of thrill ran through their beings. They began hopping, leaping and dancing out of boundless joy. When they reached the shore, they were overawed at the vast expanse of the huge mass of water. How to reach the other edge of the sea which was looking limitless, boundless and in no case negotiable. Huge waves were rising high in the sky. Their roar was sending waves of fear through the body—head to toe. The army of the monkeys and the bears sat down subdued, worried and dejected. Their spirits were dampened at the sight of the hugeness. How to go beyond was the question that was keeping them worried. Crown-prince Aṅgada used many persuasive reasons to restore their lively and spirited courage but could not show them the way out. The army of the monkeys and the bears was as huge as the sea in front of their eyes. This army could be kept stable in its place only by Aṅgada and Hanumāna.

Aṅgada summoned all the leaders of the troops of the monkeys and sleuths of bears and addressed them:

"Brothers! all of you are brave warriors of matchless courage and zeal. The movement of each one of you remains unhindered. From amongst you who can go beyond the sea, reach Laṅkā, meet Sītā and return?"

The question quietened the monkeys and the bears. After some moments, a monkey called Gaja came out with the statement, "I can leap ten Yojanas." Similarly Gavākṣa said, twenty, Śarabha, thirty, Riṣabha, forty, Gandhamādana, fifty, Mainda, sixty, Dvivida, seventy and Suṣeṇa upto eighty yojanas. Jāmbavan, the aged, said, "formerly, when I was young, I could cover a very long distance. But now I am devoid of that power. Still, I feel that the mission of the son of Kauśalyā, as ordered by king Sugrīva, cannot be ignored, neglected or given up. It has to be carried out. In this old age I can cover upto ninety yojanas in one leap. In the period gone by, when Lord Srivikrama incarnated, I had circumambulated his foot, which was equal to the size of the earth, twenty–one times. But now it is beyond my capacity to cross this vast sea. Aṅgada said, "I can certainly leap across the sea but I am not sure of returning." The aged Jāmbavān was apt in the use of the language. Praising him he said, "You are capable of carrying out the mission, but you are our leader. It would be improper to send you away. You are to be protected in every way." The reply saddened Aṅgada. He responded saying, "It seems impossible to reach the other edge of the sea. We should now abstain from food, await in the sitting posture the approach of death." Assuring Aṅgada Jāmbavān looked towards him and said, "Not that, my son! the work of Śrī Rāma will certainly be completed." Consoling Aṅgada, Jambavan looked aside towards Hanumāna jī. He was keeping utter silence. Jāmbavān knew about the curse on him. He knew his capability. He understood that he was like a coal burning within but covered with a layer of ash. His body carried the quality of Vajra, the unfailing weapon of Indra. He does not remember the infinite power that he commands. Had it not been the case, how could he sit quiet when his master Sugrīva was restless in the depth of his being for his inability to carry out and complete the mission of Śrī Rāma till this time. Jāmbavān further contemplated that he was unaware of his limitless power.

With an objective of reminding him of his powers, he said to Hanumāna, "You are an ardent devotee of Śrī Rāma. Your body is as strong and powerful as the weapon of Indra. You are born only to accomplish the work of Śrī Rāma. Why are you sitting quiet? O great warrior! you are the son of the God of wind. You have been fed on the milk of Añjanā. In your infancy, mistaking the Sun for a ripe fruit you had sprung up from the cradle and reached the Sun in one leap. Brahmā and other Gods endowed you with extraordinary boons. O the great and brave! the son of Kesarī! You are empowered with boundless and infinite might. This vast sea is nothing for you. Rise up, leap over it and reach Laṅkā. There have a vision of mother Sītā and return in no time. Save our lives, the lives of the monkeys and bears. You are the abode of the power of discernment and knowledge. The large horde of monkeys and bears, dejected and depressed due to worry and anxiety, look up to you in hope."

Having listened to the words of Jāmbavān, Hanumāna, who was absorbed in the contemplation of God, instantaneously recalled his powers and began reliving them at once. His body assumed the dimensions of a mount. Experiencing unlimited power and might, he roared in a terrifying magnitude. The roar reverberated the earth, the sky, and the regions.

Hanumāna jī assumed the dimensions of a mount of gold. Roaring, he addressed his monkey fellows: "Brothers! By the mercy of God I am ready to go beyond the regions of the celestial bodies, the planets and the stars. I may dry up the oceans if I will so, split the earth into two, jumping off their peaks, reduce the mounts to dust, this tiny sea is insignificant for me. Tell me what I should do. If you order me so, I go to Laṅkā, uproot it, lift it up and drown it in the sea and bring mother Sītā here. If you tell me, and I burn Laṅkā with Rāvaṇa aflame and turn everything therein into ash. Or tell me, I will rope Rāvaṇa by the throat, pull him down and consign him to the feet of the Lord. Or, having viewed the mother of the creation, the daughter of Janaka jī. I return here."

The words of the powerful Hanumāna jī pleased Jāmbavān immensely. He then spoke to him, "You have the capability to accomplish any task. But, you are Lord's messenger on a mission. You just have a look of mother Sītā and return with her message. After that Lord Śrī Rāma would go there and emancipate the devils and their clans. His renown will spread far and wide. We all will be fulfilled for having been the instruments of his mission. We, all the monkeys and the bears, depend on you for our energy. You return soon. May God be with you on your way through the sky."

Pleased by the blessing of the aged monkeys and the bears, Hanumāna, the embodiment of great power, the crusher of the enemy, the messenger of Śrī Rāma, in a giant leap, reached the peak of the mount Mahendra. With the powerful pressure under his feat, the mount began to go down its base. With it began the dislodgement of the peaks and trees on them. Rolling down the slope the boulders and trees caused devastation all around. Wild beasts, birds, snakes and other creatures in large number were crushed under them. At that time he looked like a huge mountain, his face looked golden and charming as that of Āruṇa, the charioteer of the Sun God. His arms assumed an unusual length and they looked like the celestial mythological snake.

Ready to take the leap, Hanumāna jī, his face towards the east, revered his father, God of wind, remembered Lord Śrī Rāma and spoke to fellow monkeys and bears: "My dear brothers! By the benevolence of Śrī Rāma I will fly like his never failing arrow, reach Laṅkā, view mother Sītā and return. At the time of his demise, a person, remembers His name, crosses the sea of the life and death and reaches the other shore without pains and troubles. I am His messenger. The divine ring of His finger is with me, his name is scribed on it, his image is in my bosom and the name is on my tongue. If I cross this tiny sea and realise fulfillment of life, what impossible will be there? Nothing. All will go as is desired. Śrī Rāma is with you and with me. He will favour us."

At that time there was an immense and unique flush of vigour, power and brilliance in the being of Hanumāna. The Gods began shouts of victory and the sages, chants of peace.

Hanumāna extended his both arms towards the south, took a powerful leap into the sky and began to fly with the powerful superspeed of Garuda. Pulled by his speed, countless trees began flying alongwith all their branches. The flowers of the flowering trees rained over him like the showers of flowers, as if venerating him.

When the sea perceived Hanumāna speeding on the mission of Śrī Rāma he thought that, "the family of Ikṣvāku, swelled my being to these dimensions, as I am now, and this fearless Hanumāna, having the body as mighty as the vajra, the weapon of Indra, is flying over me on the mission of Śrī Rāma the descendent of the same family as that of the king Sāgara, I should provide for him some respite on the way".

The sea spoke to the mount Maināka, "O great among the mounts, behold that this Hanumāna, the son of the monkey Kesarī, is speeding for Laṅkā to accomplish the mission of Śrī Rāma. The descendents of the family of the Wind are venerable for me. They are extremely venerable for you. Therefore, you please, help Hanumāna. You please raise your one peak above the level of my water, so that he can have some respite on his long journey to Laṅkā."

The Maināka, with its many peaks of gold and gems, emerged considerably up and above the sea level. Assuming the form of a human being, it stood up at one of its peaks and entreated Hanumāna, "O the best among the monkeys, you are the son of Vayu, the God of the wind, like your father you are endowed with limitless might and strength. You are erudite in the scriptures. Veneration to you will amount veneration to the God of Wind, your father. Thus, you are definitely venerable to me. Formerly the mountains enjoyed the facility of flying on wings. They flew here and there in the sky speedily. Their free and unhindered flight frightened the Gods, the sages and all the creatures. Angry on this count, the thousand eyed Indra severed the wings of lakhs of mounts. Enraged Indra, flourishing his weapon, rushed towards me. But your great and reverable father, the distinguished soul, Vayu, the God of Wind dropped me in the sea. Thus I was saved".

Treating him with esteem and affection the mount Maināka further stated, "O the source of delight to your father, Vāyu, the God of Wind! this is my sacred relation with you. You are worthy of my reverence, Besides, the sea too has commanded me to provide some respite for you and to request you to treat yourself to the various kinds of sweet fruits. Rest for a while, then proceed on your mission".

The son of Añjanā responded to the mount in an extremely affectionate speech, "Mainaka! I am immensely pleased to meet you. I have been accorded a very warm welcome and it is complete now. I want to hurry on my mission. Therefore, rest is impossible for me."

Hanumāna jī touched the person of Mainaka and speeded hurriedly ahead. At that time, both the sea and the mount, appreciated him in high esteem and sincere love, and blessed him time and over.

The Gods, viewing him speeding towards Laṅkā on the mission of Śrī Rāma, wanted to fathom his wisdom and estimate his might. They deputed Surasā, the mother of serpents, to carry out the job. Accordingly she assumed a very ugly, terrific and loathsome figure. Her eyes were yellow and pointed. She, obstructing his way, stood up in front of him. Her mouth was open and terrifying.

Watching him advancing towards herself the mother of serpents addressed him:

"O wise! I am dying of hunger. Gods have sent you as my food. You come into my mouth so that I satiate my hunger."

Hanumāna replied, "Mother! accept my veneration. I am on my mission to Laṅkā in the service to Śrī Rāma, the defender of the weak. This time you let me proceed ahead in the search for Sītā. After I return and apprise Śrī Rāma of the whereabouts of Sītā, I will fly straight into your mouth."

But, Surasā was not in any way prepared to let him proceed further. She had been assigned by the Gods to judge the calibre of Hanumāna jī. Then he volunteered himself to be eaten by her. He said to her, "All right, You consume me now."

Surasā expanded her mouth upto one yojana. The son of the God of Wind swelled his body to the dimensions of eight yojanas. She further doubled these dimensions to sixteen yojanas. Then the son of the God of Wind assumed the dimensions of thirty two yojanas. Hanumāna jī always doubled the dimensions of his body as to the dimensions of her mouth. When her mouth touched the extreme limit of a hundred yojanas, Hanumāna jī reduced himself to the size of his thumb and entered her mouth.

Surasā was about to close her jaws when Śhrī Hanumāna came out of her mouth and with hands folded in politeness said to her, "Mother I have come out of your mouth. I am on a mission of Śhrī Rama. Please, let me proceed further."

Surasā was deputed by Gods to test the calibre of Śrī Ḥanumāna. She realised that his capabilities were infinite. She allowed him on his mission with a hearty blessing for success.

Surasā left for heavens and Śrī Hanumana jī speeded towards Laṅkā. He was flying with the force of Garuda when he was encountered by a lady demon. She was Siṁhikā. She possessed the power to attract a flying bird or an object by its shadow and devour it. She caught the shadow of Śrī Hanumāna and pulled him down into her mouth. Śrī Hanumāna felt the opposite force and took some time to realise that he was being pulled down by some demonic creature in the ocean below. He jumped down over her with a force and weight which she could hardly bear. She was crushed to nullity.

Seeing the supernatural deed of Śrī Hanumāna jī, the creatures in the sky showered him with praises saying, "O great among the monkeys, you have finished this lady demon with no effort. This is an extraordinary achievement on your part. You now proceed on your mission in Laṅkā. Those who are endowed with the qualities of perseverance, wisdom, intelligence and prowess, never fail in their mission. Go ahead, success awaits you in Laṅkā. Listening to such praises and counsels, he was dashing toward Laṅkā.

In no time he was at the beach. The landscape was full of plants, trees, shrubs and creepers laden with flowers and fruits of various descriptions. There the bees were humming. The birds were cooing and the creatures roaming and playing leisurely in the sunshine. The bracing breeze was gently blowing ruffling the attires of ladies enjoying themselves in company or singly.

There he saw Laṅkā situated on the mount Trikūta. It was surrounded with a high wall and deep ditches around. He surveyed the land with a view that a war with Rāvaṇa was inevitable. The fort seemed impregnable.

There should be sufficient open land for the army to camp and storm the enemy positions. There should be a suitable place for the Lord to stay. Water and food should be available in proximity and should be easily accessible. With these and such thoughts in the mind, he contemplated that with the size of a giant as he is, it won't be proper to try to enter the fort during broad daylight. He decided to have an adventure at night.

After dusk, he sprang over the wall, assumed a smaller form, became invisible and entered the precincts of the fort of Laṅkā. The fort was too strong to be taken lightly. The defense was impregnable. All the gates or doors were of gold. The courts at each gate were paved with sapphire; the pathways were neatly kept and meticulously defended. The lakes were brimming with crystal clear water. The layout and workmanship showed that it was designed and crafted by artisans of great calibre, not lower than that of Viśwakarmā.

The security men were furious and wore a fearsome look. They roamed about and combed the entire area thoroughly all through day and night. Under these circumstances, it was not easy even for Hanumāna jī to penetrate into the system. He assumed almost an invisible look and entered the precincts. Still he was perceived by the presiding demoness—Laṅkinī. Hanumāna had mastered the supernatural powers—all eight in number—and had offered prayer at the holy feet of Śrī Rāma in his mind and memory, before embarking on his plans to be executed in Laṅkā. Even then he could not and did not escape the sight of Laṅkinī, the presiding demoness of the fort of Laṅkā. She challenged him and wanted to know his identity.

The great monkey at once realised that dispute with the demoness at this juncture of time was risky and therefore hardly advisable. Without exchanging a word, he hit her softly with a left fist as she was a woman and hitting her with full force and power of the right hand was against norms of bravery and valour. But, it was the fist of the bolt. She succumbed and crumbled on the ground instantly. She vomitted blood through nose and mouth and breathed her last through an open mouth.

Before that she told Hanumāna, "O messenger of Śrī Rāma, as you have crossed the ocean around Laṅkā, you have in a way conquered it. Rāvaṇa has caused agony to Sītā, the virtuous lady. He will suffer defeat at the hands of Śrī Rāma who has come to the mother earth to lighten the burden of evil demons. They will shortly come to an end. Fortunately, I have enormously benefitted from my association with a devotee of Śrī Rāma, though for a brief period, but before death. I feel fulfilled today. May Rāma ever dwell in my heart."

When Laṅkinī was breathing her last, Sītā experienced an auspicious omen and Rāvaṇa, an inauspicious. Śrī Rāma also experienced an auspicious omen.

Tulsidasji blessed by ParamGuru Hanumanji
Jay Jay Jay Hanuman Gosai,
Kripa Karo Guru Dev Ki Nai

Hanumāna in the Palace of Ravaṇa

Hanumāna was extremely worried about Sītā jī. He was in Laṅkā and was not able to know her whereabouts. He had not met her earlier. How could he isolate her from other ladies in Laṅkā, was the cause of his worry. Although he was in the town, he did not know the exact location where Sītā jī was kept. It was not easy even for him to identify the place of her captivity. He was closely viewing the palaces, council halls, stables, army settlements, administrative offices and the residential apartments of officers and subordinates. All the buildings, roads and pathways were closely guarded by the security men with very furious and repulsive features. He roamed the terraces, the gardens, places of amusement and entertainment. He encountered demons under the impact of hard drinks. All this enterprise was possible only for Hanumāna as he was endowed with the power to assume the form of his choice as suited the occasion and purpose.

Hanumāna entered the palace of Rāvaṇa. He was amazed at the sight of the decorative items and the items of luxury. Rāvaṇa had only one aim in his life—to satiate the hunger for sensuous pleasures. He was also whimsical in matters of his choice. He had a fancy for gold, pearls, gems and ivory. His dwelling place was covered with gold plates. It was strictly guarded by sturdy and alert men of high stature. The guards were equipped with weapons and impenetrable armour on chests and plates on arms and wrists. Their thighs and knees were also well covered. Their heads were covered with very strong helmets.

The floors were paved with sapphire. He must have a strong liking for beautiful women. Hanumāna jī saw many ladies around Rāvaṇa's bed of ivory, which was studded with precious gems—diamonds and rubies. The women wore very exquisitely crafted attires and shining ornaments of gems and pearls. They were discharging various duties assigned to them. Some were musicians, others had the duty to fan him. At the hour when Hanumāna was in the palace, all the women were tired. Some were asleep and many were half asleep. They were lying on lawns and footpaths. Their eyes were half closed due to the impact of hard drinks that they had taken. They were not conscious about their dresses. Their shapely body parts were visible through their attires ruffled by the gentle breeze. The shining pearl and diamond necklaces, gold bracelets of diamonds and rubies and armlets on their shapely arms were visible. Hanumāna saw a very graceful lady asleep on a majestic bed of ivory. He inferred that she must have been Mandodari as she was the lone person on such a precious bed and in such luxurious cushions. She was the most beautiful and graceful of all the women around. Her ornaments and dress were exquisitely crafted.

Hanumāna could not identify Sītā jī among the ladies there. His inference was that she could not have been among such ladies as were seen there. Before coming to Rāvaṇa's palace she must have died of her will. Nor she would be attired in such clothes as those women wore.

Hanumāna guessed that the women there were not forcibly brought by Rāvaṇa because they all were living in harmony and peace. They had come to the palace out of their choice or will. They were from renowned families and had opted to be there, because of Rāvaṇa's qualities of character. There were no ladies who loved a man other than Rāvaṇa or were wives of other persons before coming to Rāvaṇa's palace:

"Na canyakamapi na canya pūravā
vina varārhām janakatamajam tu"

[Va.Rāma. S./10/70]

न चान्याकामापि न चान्यपूर्वा
विना वराईम् जनकात्मजाम् तु

(वा.रा.सु. १०/७०)

Only Sītā was the lady whose husband was a man other than Rāvaṇa and who had been forcibly brought by him.

Hanumāna saw many ladies, sleeping or awake but they were all carefree. For a while a thought crept up in his mind that being a celibate, he had closely perceived the faces and other parts of the ladies whose attires were ruffled by the breeze and thus had committed a kind of sin. But the next moment he assured himself that his intentions were not vile as he was on a sacred mission of finding Sītā jī out. Nor did his mind ever deviate from the path of the razor's edge. All through the exercise, he maintained himself stable and his mind did not waver. His celibay was unbroken.

Hanumāna was eagerly longing to have a view of Sītā jī soon as the night hours were passing. He was hiding himself from the sight of the gigantic demons on duty around. Yet having scanned every nook and corner of the palace, he was not able to sight her.

He had roamed the other areas of the fort of Laṅkā also. After all, Laṅkā was not a small area. He surveyed almost the whole of it but to his dismay, Sītā did not come to his sight. He roamed the parks, orchards and gardens and places where the laity and celebrities lived. But Sītā was to be found nowhere.

Hanumāna Meets Vibhīṣaṇa

During the course he sighted a mansion the walls of which were scribbled with Rāma Nāma. At the door were the images of the weapons of Śrī Rāma, a bow and an arrow. The Tulsī shrub was planted near the temple in the courtyard of the mansion. Hanumāna jī was surprised at the sight of a dwelling which was standing alone and aloft in contrast with the neighbourhood in quality and character. When he was contemplating over the sight, he saw Vibhīṣaṇa, the inmate of the mansion, reciting the name of Śrī Rāma. The time was the last quarter of the night.

Hanumāna jī felt assured that the person was a devotee of Śrī Rāma. He assumed the guise of a Brāhmaṇa and began repeating the name of the Lord. Hearing the name, Vibhīṣaṇa came out and encountered him who was in the guise of a Brāhmaṇa. He enquired about the person and the purpose. With this curiosity in mind, he lay prostrate at the feet of the Brāhmaṇa.

Hanumāna jī gave out that he was the servant of Śrī Rāma. He was in Laṅkā on a mission of finding the whereabouts of Sītā jī, his spouse.

Hearing this, Vibhīṣaṇa felt an upsurging emotion in his chest. His eyes brimmed with tears and his voice choked in his throat. He apprised him of his birth in a class of demons. Expressing his sentiment about his life and living, he further stated that as his mind was impure, he was unable to dedicate himself to the service of the Lord.

Hanumāna jī felt extremely happy when he met Vibhīṣaṇa. He exalted him saying that, "love for Rāma, the Lord, comes to the chosen souls only. All the Gods, demigods, the sages and the great ascetics aspire in the core of their being to enjoy a dip, only one dip, in the lake of the bliss of his devotion. But all are not favoured. Vibhīṣaṇa! you are very fortunate that you are a dedicated devotee of Śrī Rāma. Certainly you are a chosen and favoured soul. You will soon enjoy the fulfillment of your life and that would be final. Lord Rāma wants only a true love and once it is there he cares for his devotees."

About himself he said that he was born as a monkey and Śrī Rāma accepted him as his devotee or a servant. He never takes into account the fact of ones birth or qualities. He is his who loves him with a true heart.

Hanumāna and Vibhīṣaṇa remained engrossed in the conversation for long. They forgot everything about their beings, their bodies and their surroundings. Suddenly they became aware of themselves and the mission of Hanumāna jī, his adventure across the sea, came up in their mind.

Hanumāna jī requested Vibhīṣaṇa to tell him the whereabouts of Sītā jī if he knew. He emphasised that he had to complete his mission as early as possible. His fellow monkeys and bears were looking for his return with expectations and that after the sunrise it would not be possible for him to go around as he would become visible to the suspecting eyes of the demons on guard. Hanumāna jī prayed then that he should be given a clue to the place where Rāvaṇa had kept her.

Vibhīṣaṇa then told him that there was a grove called Aśhoka Vātikā which was very close to the palace of Rāvaṇa and was his favourite wood.

The grove was full of trees and plants bearing juicy fruits and flowers.

In the center of the grove there is a temple dedicated to Lord Śiva. It is very majestic and grand in architectural design. There was a clear water lake around this temple. Very able male soldiers and well known lady soldiers were employed to guard the place during day and night.

Not far removed from this temple there was a tall Aśhoka tree. In the shade of this tree Sītā jī shed tears all the time. She suffers the agony of separation from her Rāma Candra jī. Her long black hair has matted into a thick mass. She has given up food and water and her body has become pale yellow in complexion. She covers her body with dirty rag of a saree only.

Very cruel and fierce ladies terrorise her all day and night. It was very difficult to reach near her. My wife and the eldest daughter Kala sometimes reached her, and said some words of consolation. I shudder at the very thought of her condition. There were armed soldiers guarding the place. Please go into the wood cautiously.

The description of the condition of Sītā jī rant the being of Hanumāna jī with emotion of sorrow. He assured Vibhīṣaṇa of the power of Śrī Rāma and expressed his confidence of meeting Sītā jī.

At the Feet of Sītā Jī

Hanumāna jī did not face any obstacle or difficulty in reaching the Aśhoka Vāṭikā. He did not cast a glance over the temple or lake and reached straight at the Aśoka tree. He hid himself in the thick foliage of the tree. He beheld Sītā jī, the brilliant embodiment of the virtue with steadfast and unwavering faith. Her eyes were downcast and were shedding tears. The viewing of Sītā jī rent the entire being of Hanumāna jī with supreme happiness. He told himself that his incarnation and its purpose were fulfilled that day as he had succeeded in his mission as an instrument of Śrī Rāma jī.

He heard some noise coming from a distance. Rāvaṇa was coming towards Sītā jī. A retinue of demon ladies and his wife Mandodarī was in his attendance. Hearing the noise, Ṣītā jī shuddered at it and tried to shroud her person unsuccessfully.

Reaching close to Sītā jī, Rāvaṇa addressed her saying that she had no reason to fear him. He loved her immensely, more than his own life. Her agony was unbearable to him. Rāma stood no comparison with him as he had vanquished Gods and had conquered the heaven itself. He had lifted up the mount Kailāśa also. The Gods dreaded him, what to say of demiGods nāgas and kinnaras, etc. This Laṅkā is situated at the mount Trikūta. It was impregnable for any enemy. Not even a bird could fly into its defence system. How could Rāma, the hermit, cover the vast ocean, an expanse of a hundred yojanas, and reach this impregnable Laṅkā? What had you to do with him who was so imbecile, powerless and lonely. I could forcibly take you to my bed.

But as I love and admire you, I did not want to agonise your mind. You concede to my exhortation and come to my side willingly.

Sītā did not budge from her conviction. Angered, Rāvaṇa tried his best to frighten her and to make her concede to his urge. But all in vain. Frightening words and ways had no impact on the firm mind of Sītā jī. Taking his sword out of its sheath, he flourished it at her as a threatening gesture and said that one stroke of this mighty sword would sever her head off her sholders and that her flesh will he consumed by the vultures and crows.

The evil speech of Rāvaṇa could not have any impact on the mind of Sītā. She kept a straw before her and with downcast eyes, rebuffed instantly his threats and said, "O vile and wicked soul, you do what you want to do. You cannot frighten me with your meaningless pronouncements. I am the wife of a great hero, Śrī Rāma Candra and in no respect you match with him. You gurgle out empty words till Rāma Candra sets his foot on the land of Laṅkā and punish you for your evil acts of theft and treachery. The arrows of Śrī Rāma will shear your limbs off your body. Then only will you realise how powerful he is. All the members of your family and your entire clan will meet their end in the battle with Śrī Rāma."

The words of Sītā jī provoked Rāvaṇa out of his wits and he rushed towards her to attack her with his flourished sword.

Mandodarī fell at his feet and implored him desperately saying, "Lord spare this lady of the human clan. She is frail, helpless and suffering. Many charming ladies of Nāga and Gandharva clans long to have you as husband. She is no match with them."

The words of Mandodarī calmed Rāvaṇa to a limit. He again addressed her saying, "You make up your mind in one month. If you do not accept me as your man in that period of grace, I will severe your head with my sword."

Before leaving the place, he exhorted the lady demons

to frighten Sītā to submit to his will within one month and that on the thirty-first day she should be cooked and served to him with his breakfast. With this caution uttered, he left the place.

The evil women of demonic clan started frightening Sītā jī. An old lady named Trijaṭā tried to dissuade them from torturing Sītā jī. She said that they were definitely going to meet their disaster by torturing an innocent lady such as Sītā. She, in order to dissuade them from their evil design of torturing Sītā , narrated her dream in which she visualised Rāvaṇa with his shaven head, "I saw that he had bathed with oil and was putting on red clothes. Also I saw him falling from the pushpak and going towards the south on the back of an ass. I also saw Meghanāda, Kumbhakarṇa and generals of the army of Rāvaṇa accompanying him in the same direction, the south. I had also seen that a monkey with a red mouth had pushed Laṅkā in a large uncontrollable inferno and that a woman was pulling Rāvaṇa in an unknown direction. All these dreams I saw in the morning and therefore are bound to come true."

This narration of the dream frightened the evil women of demonic class. They fell at the feet of Sītā jī and prayed for her forgiveness. Then they left for their abodes.

Sītā jī felt very nervous at this turn of events in her life. Dejected to the limit as she was, she exhorted Trijaṭā to fetch fire from some corner so that she could end her life by burning. In the end she burst into tears. Hanumāna jī, sitting on the branch of a tree, viewed the entire scenario. But, thinking that his sudden appearance before her might frighten her, he kept to himself. Trijaṭā did not oblige Sītā jī with fire and went home. In the meantime Sītā jī got up and showed her firm determination to end her life with a firm stranglehold around her neck with the locks of her hair. Hanumāna jī could not endure this sight. Keeping himself out of her sight, he narrated all episodes of the story of Śrī Rāma from the beginning till her separation from him. This diverted her mind a little.

He also apprised her of the agony Śrī Rāma underwent in her absence and the great effort that he made to know her whereabouts from any source. He also narrated how he killed Bālī, rescued Sugrīva from his torturous ways, and restored his wife to him. He told her that Sugrīva was helping him in his expedition for her recovery. This convinced Sītā jī of the great endeavours that Śrī Rāma jī was making to rescue and recover her from the hold of Rāvaṇa.

Sītā jī at this juncture asked Hanumāna jī to appear before her eyes so that she could behold the person who had delivered good news of consolation to her.

Hanumāna jī now descended down the tree and offered obeisance at her feet. The appearance of Hanumāna jī created a sense of awe in her mind. Hanumāna jī reassured her of the genuine plans to rescue her. He gave full details of his adventure across the vast expanse of ocean and setting foot at the soil of impregnable Laṅkā. He also narrated how large contingents of armies of monkeys and bears had been sent out to search for her. He disclosed about the gold ring of Śrī Rāma on which his name was inscribed and was emitting the rays of divinity around. In order to assure her that the days of her agony were, counted and not many, he gave out that a month's time limit had been set to report back to king Sugrīva. Failure in compliance would result in the death penalty.

The account of Śrī Rāma jī's agony of separation and the gigantic endeavour to search for her aroused her confidence in the certainty of her release from the clutches of Rāvaṇa and assured her of his final destruction at the hands of her dear Lord Rāma Candra jī.

The message that Rāma jī had sent through Hanumāna jī and which he delivered to her vocally, filled her heart with the feeling of joy and assured her that he had not forgotten her with the passage of time. She felt that her image and memory were alive in the heart of Śrī Rāma, her lord, and that the time of her release was nearing. The length of separation was unbearable for her. The brave Hanumāna jī put forth that he could upturn the foothill of Laṅkā and could carry her on his back to the other beach of the sea.

Hearing these high sounding words sent a wave of laughter on the face of Sītā jī. To establish firm confidence in the power and strength of Śrī Rāma and in his calibre, he expanded his body to gigantic dimensions. Sītā jī felt assured and re-assured of the calibre of Hanumāna jī and the success of the entire expedition for her recovery on the part of Śrī Rāma and his devout fellow generals.

Hanumāna jī further said that he was only an ordinary monkey in the service of Sugrīva but by the grace of Śrī Rāma jī he could destroy the entire clan of demons like Rāvaṇa then and there but that he was desisting from it as his Lord had not commanded him to do that.

Seeing all that he had shown and hearing all that he had spoken, Sītā jī vouchsafed him with a blessing, "O Hanumāna you will be endowed with the virtue and quality of dedication to Śrī Rāma jī and he will always be compassionate to you. You will ever remain undaunted in the face of any evil or danger. No enemy shall ever he able to defeat you in war or battle or anywhere else. You shall be the abode of all divine qualities and knowledge. Śrī Raghunatha jī will always bestow mercy on you."

Hanumāna felt fulfilled. The dust particles of Sītā jī's feet adored his face. He knew that the blessing of Sītā jī could never go futile. He felt satisfied, fulfilled and exalted.

The sense of achievement aroused some appetite and he asked for permission to go around and eat what was available in the woods. Mother Jānakī, extremely relieved as she was feeling, readily okayed his request, but cautioned against the demons around. Hanumāna jī remained unconcerned of them and sprang from branch to branch looking for juicy fruits to satiate his hunger.

In a short while the woods were in a dilapidated state.

"THAI HANUMAN"
BY TARIN YUANGTRAKUL

Devastation in Aśoka Vāṭikā

Permitted by Sītā jī to satiate his hunger, Hanumāna jī contemplated on some aspects of his expedition to Laṅkā.

He thought that he should have a complete picture of the defence system of Laṅkā which had been developed and implemented by the able generals of Rāvaṇa.

He should also assess the striking power of the enemy before his departure.

Somehow he should take some steps so that he goes into the audience with Rāvaṇa and meets him face to face.

He should roam about in the fort during the day so that he could see the fortification of the town.

Also, before returning from Laṇkā he should leave some dreadful impact on the minds of demons and break down their moral strength. He should generate a sense of security and hope in the heart of Sītā jī so that she could pass the remaining days of her captivity with some confidence in her release in near future, which was certain to happen.

All these ideas he contemplated upon.

With these thoughts and schemes in his mind and fearless determination in his heart, he climbed up a tree and plucked the fruits. Some he nibbled and many he threw away. He jumped from branch to branch. Many branches gave way under his weight and many under his force. He broke many trunks down to pieces. Many trees he jolted out of their roots and many he uprooted. He was on an uncontrollable spree of large scale destruction in the favourite woods of Rāvaṇa. He in this way threw a strong challenge to his power and might in his own land, under his nose.

The warriors, the guards, the occupants and their wives and children all were taken aback at this daring act on the part of a monkey whom none of them, singly or jointly, could hold up. Many gathered to mount an attack on him, but he could not be restrained. Some mighty power had taken him over and he was casting a spell of destruction all around over the woods and over the demons, many of whom he crushed to death and many he rendered dilapidated.

Desperate, they approached their lord, Rāvaṇa with an account of their helplessness to deal with a monkey, a red faced quadruped, and hold him up from a large scale devastation he was carrying out in a cruel way. The account of destruction in the woods rent Rāvaṇa up with the emotion of anger. He dispatched Jambumālī, the son of his minister, Prahasta, to catch the culprit and present him dead or alive in his court. Jambumālī possessed a large body and was fierce in anger. He roared in the presence of Śrī Hanumāna jī and he in one jolt broke him down to pieces.

The news infuriated Rāvaṇa beyond proportion. He deployed seven warrior sons of his ministers to hold him up. Flourishing their weapons of destruction and roaring aloud to cow him down to submit, they came up rushing towards him, but he was ready to meet them with a pole of iron, which he had uprooted from the soil and which he was holding in his hand to deliver a deadly blow onto them when they came near him to attack. The pole he wielded in such a way that they all came under its strike and they lay on the dust never to get up and breathe again.

The news of this failure rent Rāvaṇa up with impotent anger which he desperately failed to bear. He summoned his five generals and deployed them with the contingents of fiercest fighters to catch the miscreant quadruped dead or alive.

The generals dashed towards Hanumāna to deal him a deadly blow. Hanumāna jī was awaiting the attack. He roared and sprang with such fierceness as the reverberating sound rent up the skies and echoed and re-echoed all through the space. The roar of Hanumāna jī rendered them lifeless and their weapons ineffective. Wielding an iron pole he crushed the entire invading force in one counter attack.

The news upset Rāvaṇa seriously. As a last resort he deployed his brave son Akṣa Kumāra to deal with Hanumāna jī.

Seeing him rushing towards him, Hanumāna jī jumped up into the sky and came down on his chariot so heavily that the horses and the vehicle were crushed under his weight and force. Akṣa Kumāra swiftly escaped from the crumbling chariot and rushed towards him to strike with a deadly weapon. Hanumāna jī again dashed up into the sky. Akṣa chased him. Hanumāna jī caught hold of his legs, whirled him round and round thousands of times and dashed him down on the earth so violently that his limbs lost their form and figure and could not be traced. Only the streaks of blood could be seen here and there.

Rāvaṇa could not bear the agony of the untimely death of his dear and brave son. He rose up to proceed to capture Hanumāna jī himself. His son, Meghanāda, dissuaded him from the endeavour saying that he should not personally go to capture an ordinary and tiny quadruped. Such an endeavour on his part would amount to humiliation.

Seeing that Meghanāda was ready to proceed to meet Hanumāna in a sort of duel, he thought it better to caution him against underestimating the power and strength of Hanumāna. He said that, "The monkey did not seem to be an ordinary animal. He had given an extraordinary account of his unfathomable reservoir of courage and strength till then. His power knows no bounds. He seems to be the embodiment of the power of fire and was likely to foil any attempt at killing him. So remember the supernatural power and effect of your bow, endowed with divine quality, and proceed with a determination that would not go futile."

Meghanāda went round his father as a mark of obeisance and mounted his chariot. On reaching in front of Hanumāna jī, he roared aloud. Hanumāna jī, wielding the iron pole, jumped up in the sky.

Meghanāda shot a barrage of arrows at Hanumāna jī. His body oozed blood. The gigantic Hanumāna, in a frenzy of unbearable anger, wielded the iron pole and in one strike smashed his chariot and dispatched his charioteer and fellow fighters to the other world.

Meghanāda as a final resort shot the Brahma Pāsha to bind him. Though Hanumāna jī enjoyed the boon never to be subjected to the Brahma Pāsha, he thought it not improper to submit to the impact of Brahma Pāsha the weapon of the creator of the worlds. Hanumāna fell to it, as if with a will to do so.

A crowd of demons gathered around fallen Hanumāna jī. They showered him with filthy abuses. Some, who were too enthusiastic, ran home and back with all kinds of strings and ropes. They bound him and he willed submission in order to keep up the honour of Brahmā jī and his weapon. The demons bound Hanumāna jī with the ropes and as a result freed him of binding impact of Brahmā jī's Pāsha. Little did they know that the Brahma Pāsha did not work when any other binding means were resorted to. Meghanāda, seeing that Hanumāna ji was wrapped in a soft material only, lost all hope of his victory as he was aware of the condition that the Brahma Pāsha could not be used twice.

Hanumāna jī behaved as if he was still under the bondage of Brahma Pāsha and did not show up his freedom.

Meghanāda escorted him to the court of his father, Rāvaṇa, the mighty, the furious.

In the Court of Rāvaṇa

In the audience of his father Meghanāda stated, "Revered father, this inordinate quadruped has played havoc with the woods and killed many warriors of our clan. Now he is at your mercy. Justice, as envisaged by your ministers, may be meted out to him."

Hanumāna jī scanned the calibre of the ministers of Rāvaṇa quickly. They were four in numbers, two on either side of him. Their names were Durdhara, Prahasta, Mahāparśva, and Nikumbha.

The complexion of Rāvaṇa was like heated gold. He was sitting on the majestic throne of sphaṭika, a precious stone. His gold crowns were emitting glare around. Hanumāna jī viewed him respectfully although he had undergone distressing torments at the hands of demons. He thought that had he been anchored in virtue and piety, he would have been a great defender of the entire region of Gods.

Seeing Hanumāna in front of him, Rāvaṇa became furious and asked Prahasta to enquire of him who he was, why he had devastated the woods, and why he had killed his dear son and great warriors. Prahasta first tried to comfort Hanumāna jī with his words. He assured him that he would be set free soon if he spoke truth freely, frankly and fearlessly. He exhorted him to reveal who had sent him there and who he was.

Hanumāna jī had no fear whatsoever in the presence of the personage who had conquered all the three worlds. Revealing his identity he said that he was a messenger of Lord Rāma who was God incarnate on the earth to destroy the wrong doers from its face.

Reminding him of his disability even to move the bow of Lord Śiva in the assembly of the Kings at the court of Janaka jī in Mithilā, he put forth that it was Śrī Rāma alone who not only moved the bow but also stringed it and won the hand of Sītā jī.

Reminding him of his noble lineage, he said, "You come of the noble ancestry of Brahmā Jī; Kubera was your brother, Pulastya, the great sage, was your grand father. You are well versed in the Vedas and Śāstras. By birth you are noble, by the Ātman too, you are not evil, by knowledge also you are not demonic. You are ignoble only by deeds and due to your excessively egoistic nature."

"O, Rāvaṇa the mighty and the noble, you brought Sītā jī deceitfully like a thief. That did not behove you. You were underestimating the power of Śrī Rāma jī. He is the Lord Himself. His brother, Laxmaṇa jī, is the Divine Śeṣha Nāga incarnate in human form. Both of them, singly or jointly, could upturn your Laṅkā, make you and your fellow demons disappear into nil. There was none in the three worlds who could dare displease Rāma and enjoy happiness. There was none among Gods, demiGods, demons and nagas who could face him in the battle."

"My Lord, Śrī Rāma, had commanded me to go out in search for Sītā jī. I carried out an expedition of adventure across the sea and found Sītā jī in your favourite woods. It would be in the fitness of things that she was restored to her Lord with full honours. Or, prepare yourself, your kinsmen and members of your clan to meet annihilation at the hands of my Lord, Śrī Rāma. None in Laṅkā, including the soldiers and warriors, would be able to escape death."

"I warn you Rāvaṇa! Counsel you and advise you not to unmind the truth, the path of virtue and piety, but to renounce the ignoble ways of sin."

The words of Śrī Hanumāna jī infuriated him immensely. His eyes turned red with deep anger. Belching fiery words out of his mouth, he threatened him with the penalty of death to be meted out to him then and there. This did not frighten the indomitable Hanumāna. It could not.

Hanumāna's fearlessness further infuriated Rāvaṇa beyond any proportion. He fired, "How you dare open your mouth and speak out such words as you have spoken here in my presence. You tiny quadruped are not aware of my temper and power. Your Sugrīva, Rāma and Lakṣmaṇa cannot stand the brilliance that I personify. I will kill you, Sītā and everybody that you rely on and boast of and send all to the regions of yama, who with his entire retinue is a slave to me."

All this nonsense did not dislodge Hanumāna from his conviction. He retorted, "Sugrīva is my king. He is the younger brother of Bālī whose valour you are well aware of. I need not remind you of the fact that he had kept you under captivity for many months. That event might be quite alive in your memory."

This was unbearable for Rāvaṇa. He stood up pulled his sword out of sheath, flourished it and moved to attack Hanumāna.

At this moment, Vibhīṣaṇa came forward. He tried to calm down the anger of his elder brother Rāvaṇa. He said, "Brother you very well understand the Sāstras; you are also well versed in the laws of polity. The wise men hold that a messenger does not deserve a death penalty in any circumstance whatsoever. He is only a messenger. He will always speak in favour of his master. There are other options open to punish him. You can apply any of them."

Accepting the stand taken up by Vibhīṣaṇa, he said, "Yes, some other punishment but death should be meted out to him for the devastation of the woods and killing of demons. His tail is very dear to him. It should be burnt and he should be taken round the lanes and sublanes of Laṅkā, with his tail aflame". Further speaking to his men, he said, "Citizens of Laṅkā, humiliate this quadruped, burn his tail and take him round."

Laṅkā Ablaze

Hanumāna was not showing his actual size. His tail was only a short one.

Hearing the command of their king, Rāvaṇa, the citizens gathered oil and rags. They wanted to wrap the tail of Hanumāna with rags and soak it in oil. But Hanumāna jī increased the length of his tail and, went on doing so, till all the rags and the entire supply of the oil fell short of the requirement.

Then the people brought him to the main crossroads of Laṅkā. Here an officer of Rāvaṇa's army ignited the tail. Hanumāna sprang up with his tail aflame. He jumped from house top to house top and from tree top to tree top, thus turning the whole of Laṅkā aflame. All the important buildings, the residential quarters of the soldiers and warriors, the palaces of the generals and the ministers and the houses of the ordinary people came into the grip of the widescale inferno. The people came out of their burning houses to kill the quadruped who was spreading fire all around. When they wanted to shoot arrows at him they saw him at large from house top to house top. Hanumāna jī had assumed the gigantic dimensions of his body and was looking extremely frightful. The entire Laṅkā, its people and the management, sank into chaos and confusion, hitherto unknown and unheard of.

The wind gave an unprecedented speed to the fire. The gushes of the wind and the flames of the fire took the whole town into their grips. The smoke emitted by the flames turned the people blind. The army establishments too came under fire.

A lady-demon seeing the grisly state of the town ran up to Sītā jī to tell her that the monkey, she was talking to, was aflame and had caused a widespread inferno, into which the whole Laṅkā was sinking.

Sītā jī got apprehensive of the welfare and safety of Hanumāna jī and prayed to the wind to remain cool around his person and save him from the flames. The Wind God was already cautious about the well being of his son and was guarding him against the burning effect of flames.

Hanumāna jī was safe but Laṅkā was gutted.

The warriors of Rāvaṇa including Meghanāda failed to catch hold of Hanumāna jī as he was felt everywhere and was visible nowhere; whom to catch and whom not to catch?

Desperate Rāvaṇa deployed Yama and his retinue to catch and kill Hanumāna. Hanumāna jī kept Yama inside his mouth and lambasted his retinue with his enormous burning tail. They could not bear the hurt and burns and ran away.

Yama, imprisoned in the mouth of Hanumāna jī, could not discharge his duties of keeping the living world in balance equilibrium of death and birth. Hanumāna jī had assumed the form and the state of Kala, the destroyer of all. The Gods in the leadership of Brahmā jī came down to Hanumāna jī and prayed for the release of Yama so that the creation could be sustained. Yama was accorded release and he subsequently decided in his heart that he would never go near the devotees of Śrī Hanumāna jī.

Finally Rāvaṇa deployed the clouds to extinguish fire created by Hanumāna Jī. They poured enormous amount of water down on Laṅkā. But the effect was opposite. The rain of water raised the flames higher and higher. The water drops acted as drops of oil in the flames.

The clouds finally dried. The entire population of Laṅkā cried for help. But no help came from any quarter.

Hanumāna jī became apprehensive of the safety of Sītā jī. He jumped into the sea and extinguished the fire of his tail. When he came above the sea, he heard the minstrels singing. They were praising Hanumāna jī for his supernatural deed. He heard that the city of Laṅkā was rending with the cries and wailings of the women, old and young, the children and the aged. The mounts, the caves, the houses, the palaces, the concealed apartments, the terraces, the minarets, the walls, the gardens, the orchards, the groves – all were gutted to ashes. Only the residence of Vibhīṣaṇa and the place of Sītā jī where she used to sit squat or lie, were saved.

Hanumāna jī while entering the fort of Laṅkā had dislodged some stones out of their place. In that place Rāvaṇa had imprisoned Saturn. He got his release out of the hole thus made. While escaping from the hole, he looked askance and muttered, "The days left of Rāvaṇa, his kinsmen and Laṅkā were only a few."

Adieu

Hanumāna had accomplished a feat. Contented and joyous, he came out of the sea and rushed towards Sītā jī. She felt an upsurge of emotion in her bosom. Tears brimmed her eyes. She placed her hand on his head which was at her feet in obeisance.

He apprised her of his doings and achievements while in Laṅkā. He told her that he had gathered necessary information of the places in Laṅkā. He also informed her of what he had known of the fighting calibre of Rāvaṇa's forces. Also assured her of the imminent expedition of Śrī Rāma jī for her rescue.

Sītā jī enquired how the monkeys and bears could come to that shore of the ocean, small creatures endowed with limited power and strength as they were. Hanumāna jī assured her that by the grace of Śrī Rāma jī, each monkey and bear was capable of performing excessively daring feat of bravery. Nothing was impossible if the Lord willed so. And Śrī Rāma jī was in favour of demolishing Laṅkā and the rule of Rāvaṇa as he was the destroyer of virtue and piety. Also that, he had incurred the displeasure of sages and saints besides the wrath of Gods.

The reply of Hanumāna jī satisfied Sītā ji.

Hanumāna jī addressing her further stated that as Śrī Rāma jī had sent a gold ring as a token of credence, he should be favoured with something similar. Sītā jī took a precious jewel out of her hair and entrusting that to him said, "The jewel be given to Rāma. He and Lakṣmaṇa would feel reassured of your having reached me and of the fact that I was safe and alive. This would refill their hearts with courage and zeal to demolish Rāvaṇa and rescue me."

Hanumāna received the jewel, her chūḍāmaṇi, with all reverence.

Sītā jī also asked him to remind Śrī Rāma jī of an episode when he had picked up a straw from the earth and shot it towards a crow. The crow was none other than the son of Indra, in a guise. That crow was roaming in search of a morsel of flesh. He had torn the skin of my toe. When Śrī Rāma jī came to know of the incident, he shot the arrow of that straw at the crow. The weapon of straw chased the crow. None in the three worlds favoured the crow with a refuge against the unfailing weapon of Śrī Rāma. The crow lastly returned at the feet of the Lord. It had to go without one eye as a punishment for the mischief he had played on me.

"Remind my lord of his power and loving concern for me and tell him that he should invade Lanka as early as possible because I am undergoing the unbearable agony of separation", she exhorted Hanumāna jī.

Hanumāna jī sprang up and descended on a peak of Ariṣṭha Giri. There his body assumed gigantic dimensions. He roared and roared to give an expression of valour and strength.

From the peak he lept up into the sky in order to leave towards the North. The leap was so powerful that the peak caved into the earth.

Having attained the height and speed he roared and roared violently. The violent magnitude of the sound rent the skies. Consequently the quarters reverberated, the clouds shattered, the seas tided, the peaks broke apart and fell and the tremors ran up and down the whole of Laṅkā, the pregnant women aborted; Rāvaṇa himself tumbled down his throne and his courtiers also fell. His crown rolled down his head and fell on the earth. These bad omens sounded evil for Laṅkā and became the talk of the town.

Across the Sea

The roar of Hanumāna jī vibrated on this side of the sea also. Hundreds of thousand of monkeys and bears began hopping out of excitement. They took it that Hanumāna jī was returning home with the news of Sītā jī. They were awaiting his arrival with rapt expectation. They interpreted the roar as a signal of firm information of the success of the expedition across the seas. They climbed up the trees and peaks and started waving the clothes as a sign of a happy welcome to him.

He descended on a peak of a mountain. From there he jumped down onto the plain earth. Seeing him there the monkeys and bears flocked around him. He began narrating to them the episode saying, "I reached Sītā jī, touched her feet in obeisance and brought the jewel of her hair as a token of credence of the event." At this Jāmbvan held him tightly in his arms and expressed his gratitude for having saved the life of each and all.

Excited immensely, the monkeys and bears began dancing in ecstasy. They expressed their happiness in various ways. Some kissed his tail, others massaged his body. Many wanted to serve him in their own ways. Most of them hopped and danced with their tails raised. In short, all of them expressed their gratitude and appreciation in their own ways.

Hanumāna jī gave a vivid account of his flight in the sky, his encounter with the evil spirits, his rest for a while on a peak of Maināka, which it had raised out of the sea waters for his convenience and finally landing at the beach of Laṅkā.

He narrated very briefly his meeting with Vibhīṣaṇa, the clue to the living place of Sītā jī; he described the woods of Aśoka Vātikā; condition of Sītā jī, torments from Rāvaṇa and the evil women in his retinue, his (Hanumāna jī's) appearing before Sītā jī; presenting her with gold ring with the name of Rāma inscribed on it, his battles with the demons, killing of Akṣa Kumāra, the final encounter with Meghanāda and his submission to the weapon of Brahmā jī, his ultimate bondage resulting in presentation to the Rāvaṇa in his court, his furious nature and provocation at his advice to return Sītā jī to her Lord Śrī Rāma Candra jī. Rāvaṇa's anger, the punishment meted out to him by way of setting his tail aflame. He described in detail the inferno that blazed up and down Laṅkā town and gutted everything and every house that came under its sway. Adieu to Sītā jī.

Hearing all this, Aṅgada explained that he was the greatest among the monkeys in valour and strength. He expressed the hope that Rāma Candra jī's agony of separation from his spouse, Sītā jī, would shortly be over.

After this the large contingent of monkeys and bears left for the abode of Śrī Rāma Candra jī to break to him the good news of finding out the place where Sītā jī was kept in Laṅkā.

The monkeys and bears were extremely happy and excited. They had little control over their behaviour. On their way, they arrived at a forest which was guarded by Dadhimukha. He was the maternal uncle of Sugrīva. The forest was over a vast expanse of land. It was called Madhu Vana. It was beautifully laid out and meticulously maintained. The beauty and the wealth of the woods figured in the conversations very often. The sight of the woods and its closeness enticed the monkeys and bears to roam about there. Aṅgada extended permission to visit and roam about in the woods. Monkeys were monkeys after all. They were not disciplined and cultured. They devastated the whole place. Many monkeys under intoxication misbehaved with the guard. Dadhimukha, who was responsible for its maintenance, reported the matter to Sugrīva. He took it as a manifestation of the joy over the success of the expedition recovery, the mission on which contingents were sent out in all the directions. He calmed the temper of Dadhimukha and said that it appears certain that the mission on which they were sent out is successful. Otherwise Aṅgada would not have permitted monkeys to enjoy themselves with the drinks and fruit nor they would have dared to behave that way.

Rāma Candra jī overheard the conversation and wanted to know what they were talking about.

Sugrīva himself reported that it was likely that Hanumāna was successful in his mission across the sea and returned with the confirmed information about Sītā jī.

Rāma and Lakṣmaṇa became happy to hear all that. Sugrīva asked Dadhimukha to make the contingent move swiftly and arrive there shortly. Dadhimukha conveyed the command to Aṅgada, Hanumāna and Jāmbavān. They flew up in the sky and reached the destination in no time. Their contingents too followed them.

Śrī Rāma Candra jī was camping at the mount Prasaravaṇa Giri. Lakṣmaṇa had constructed a hut of leaves and stalks. Rāma Candra jī was sitting in front of this hut. Lakṣmaṇa was attending on him. Sugrīva was sitting beside him.

He saw the flying squads of monkeys and bears approaching towards him. He conveyed to Śrī Rāma Candra jī that Hanumāna had the firm news of the whereabouts of Sītā jī and was to land there in no time, alongwith the fellow monkeys. Aṅgada and Jāmbavān were also with him. He tried to calm down the upsurge of emotion in his heart at the sudden breaking of the news.

At the same time the contingent under the leadership of Hanumāna landed and roared in the excitement of joy.

The monkeys lay prostrate at the feet of Śrī Rāma Candra jī, Lakṣmaṇa and Sugrīva. Hanumāna jī came forward and stated that Sītā jī was observing the norms of a virtuous lady meticulously and had become very lean. But she was in good health.

He said that he had met her in person. Folded hands, he looked at the face of Śrī Rāma Candra, his eyes reveted thereon. He waited for questions of enquiry.

Śrī RāmachandraRāma Candra enquired of him about the land where Sītā jī was and how she felt about him (Śrī Rāma Candra). He eagerly wanted to know all about her.

Hanumāna jī politely and humbly stated, "On the other shore of 100 yojana wide sea was situated the fort of Laṅkā in the South, ruled over by Rāvaṇa. The fort is inhabited by the evil demons. In that fort I saw her under an Aśoka tree suffering the agony of separation. I found her shedding tears and remembering you all the time. She was like a fish out of water. Her agony was beyond words."

Further describing her state and condition, he narrated that, "She slept on the ground. Constantly she was under the guard of evil demonic women. She scarcely took water and food. I saw her under great suffering. As a token of credence she parted with her ornament, the Cūḍamaṇi, of her hair and handed over to me for presenting it to you. Her unkempt hair is matted into a thick mass."

Hanumāna jī said that Sītā also remembered the episode of Jayanta, the son of Indra, in the guise of a crow, against whom he had shot an arrow of straw to penalise him for the mischief he had played with her and had asked me to remind you of the same.

That she told me only to remind you of your immense power and to motivate you for action against Rāvaṇa, the evil doer.

Taking the Cūḍamaṇi in his hand, Śrī Rāma Candra pressed it against his heart lovingly and fondly, remembered that the ornament was accorded to his father–in-law by Indra. At the time of his marriage, he presented Sītā jī with that Cūḍamaṇi. She used to wear it on the parting of her hair.

Rāma Candra jī felt immensely grateful to Hanumāna jī as he had accomplished the task which was beyond the power of even Gods to do. He held Hanumāna jī close to his person, in his arms. He expressed his appreciation saying that he was his very dear and closest devotee.

Hanumāna jī felt satisfied as his mission of his incarnation as a monkey was fulfilled that day.

Then, Śrī Rāma Candra jī enquired in detail as to how he crossed the sea, entered the impregnable fort of Laṅkā, roamed around the roads and woods of the town, inhabited only by demons, how he met Sītā jī and the message she sent for Lakṣmaṇa and himself.

Hanumāna jī narrated all that had happened in detail.

He narrated that Sītā jī was apprehensive about his bona fide identity. The gold ring with Rāma inscribed on it created confidence in her mind.

She told me, "Son, tell my Lord how I am being tormented by these evil women."

"In order to restore her composure" Hanumāna told Śrī Rāma jī, "I said to her that Śrī Rāma was an ocean of unlimited power and strength and no later than he came to know your whereabouts, he would invade Laṅkā and free you of the captivity of Rāvaṇa."

Sītā jī asked me to convey to Lakṣmaṇa her sincere regrets for the harsh words she had uttered to him before Rāvaṇa took her forcibly away from the hut.

She also sent her blessings to all the clans of monkeys and bears especially to Aṅgada, Jāmbvān and Sugrīva jī. She hoped that soon their armies would invade Laṅkā and destroy the regime of evil and sin.

Hanumāna jī described at length the fortification of Laṅkā. There was a high wall of gold all around the town. The deep ditches full of water and aquatic predators surround walls of the fort. Across the ditches are built strong bridges on which are installed the machines which throw off the enemy soldiers as soon as they set their foot over them. It was rather impossible to invade Laṅkā.

The fort has four gates in all the four quarters. On the eastern gate are deployed ten thousand fierce fighters; on the southern gate there are one lakh demon fighters, supported by all the four wings of the army, deployed there. The western gate is guarded by 10 lakh soldiers; the northern gate is protected by the 10 crore soldiers. The central cantonment is protected by hundreds of thousands of soldiers. Laṅkā is covered by the guns which belch fire with shells. But by the grace of my Lord I succeeded in demolishing the entire fortification. The gates are smashed, ditches are levelled and the walls are downed. One–fourth of the demonic army I have already demolished. The whole of town is a heap of ash as a result of the widespread and large-scale inferno for which they themselves were responsible. Now terror has taken over the administration of Laṅkā. Hanumāna opined that was the proper time to march.

Śrī Rāma Candra told Sugrīva that as the auspicious conjuction of stars, styled by the learned as the Victory, Vijay, was passing, the armies should the ordered to march towards South.

At once the word of comand went round the army settlement and the soldiers came out of their·quarters to fall in line and march towards Laṅkā.

Armies marched day and night. They shouted, "Victory to Śrī Rāma."

Śrī Rāma was on the shoulders of Hanumāna and Lakṣmaṇa on those of Aṅgada. Gaja, Gavākṣa, Manida, Dvivida, Nala, Nīla, Suṣeṇa and Jāmbavān were continously watching all-round and controlling the movement which was gigantic and unprecedented in human memory.

Sītā jī felt an auspicioius omen as the army marched.

Soon the armies reached the shore of the vast blue sea. Soldiers rent the air with shouts of "Victory to Śrī Rāma, Victory to Śhri Lakṣmaṇa."

The roar of the soldiers outdid that of the sea waves.

Compassion on Vibhīṣaṇa

The populace of Laṅkā, having heard the news of the arrival of a large army of monkeys and bears with a design to attack Laṅkā, became restless. Their apprehension was magnified multifold, by the idea that when a single monkey could carry out devastation on such a wide and large scale as the town had witnessed, what could be the extent of devastation if the number of monkeys was one million. Such was the terror in their mind.

Rāvaṇa too was taken over by fear as he had already witnessed the extraordinary expression of valour and strength when Hanumāna had made his presence felt in such a devastating way only a few day ago. But it was below his egoistic dignity to concede to it in the assembly of his ministers and courtiers. Displaying his usual aggressive anger, he asked for advice as to how to mete out a crushing punishment to these vile humans and mischievous quadrupeds.

The flatterers played the same old music of his victory over the Gods, demi-Gods and humans and tried to appease his ego. They said that the solo monkey could do what it did because they were not prepared and were taken by surprise, but this time those monkeys who had come with a design to invade Laṅkā shall not be allowed to return to their abodes. Instead they all will be dispatched to the regions of death. The earth would be made free of those menacing monkeys. "They would not be able to withstand your flying arrows resembling snakes with divided tongues. They would be wiped out of the face of the earth. Let us invade the other shore and demolish their strength." These flatterers said this to Rāvaṇa and the assembly of ministers and courtiers.

Rāvaṇa's end was approaching fast. These talks pleased him immensely. But Vibhīṣaṇa, his younger brother, who listened to these counsels with a strong disapproval in his mind, stood up, moved forward a little and expressed his opinion which ran contrary to the suggestions made by the short sighted flatterers.

He said, "These ministers find it easy to flatter you because they crave for personal gains. Little do they care for the good of their Lord, his kins and the populace of Laṅkā."

"Lord, you are a brave warrior, you have fought many battles and conquered even the Gods what to say of humans and animals. Did you ever think of a solo monkey coming all the way across the vast sea and reverting the impregnable defence system of the fort, that Laṅkā was, and reaching the meticulously guarded woods of Aśoka Vāṭika and besides meeting Sītā, could kill innumerable demons alongwith your brave son Akṣa Kumāra. Later he appeared in your presence and remained undaunted. What followed is not unknown to you. The whole of Laṅkā including the military establishments were burnt down to ashes."

"These were the premonitions to something that is going to happen to Laṅkā and the demonic clan. It was evidently obvious that the enemy forces had conjoined to bring about a crumbling devastation onto the race we all belong to."

"See, we should guard against the falling evil, not invite it. We should return virtuous Sītā, the perfect epitome of the highest qualities of womanhood."

Infuriated Rāvaṇa, stood up, came down from his throne, walked up to Vibhīṣana and hit him with his foot.

Vibhīṣaṇa fell down from his seat. Not feeling humiliated and maintaining his composure, he addressed Rāvaṇa, his hands folded in reverence, "you are my elder brother, just like my revered father. I do not want to see you being killed at the hands of Śrī Rāma whom the whole creation adores. I leave your court, Laṅkā and everything that I have here and proceed to the other shore of the sea".

Vibhīṣaṇa came out of the fort of Laṅkā. His four ministers accompanied him. All came by the sky route.

The monkey soldiers perceived him from a distance, took him for a spy of Rāvaṇa. At once they arrested him and presented him in the audience of Śrī Sugrīva. Having known that the person in custody was no other than the mighty brother of the enemy Rāvaṇa, he approached Śrī Rāma for commands about him, saying, "Lord! Brother of Rāvaṇa has come to your feet. Please, command me as to what should be meted out to him who has come from the enemy ranks."

Śrī Rāmachandra asked Sugrīva for his opinion. He gave his opinion by saying that the demons were evil spirits. They exercised some powers, which were contrary to the path of Dharma. They could become invisible also. He was the brother of Rāvaṇa, our enemy. He should not be trusted and should be done away with immediately. His ministers too should not be spared.

Hearing the words of Sugrīva, Hanumāna felt aggrieved. He knew the qualities of Vibhīṣaṇa. He had met him in Laṅkā. He had given the clue to the whereabouts of Sītā jī. He had spoken in Hanumāna's favour in the court of Rāvaṇa. Now, Hanumāna kept quiet and waited for the response from Śrī Rāma.

Śrī Rāma did not favour the stand taken by Sugrīva. He held that even if an enemy sought protection, he should be accorded a welcome and refuge in every case. "I grant protection to the sinners even if they murdered Brāhmanas or slaughtered the cows, provided they came to me and sought refuge with a clear heart. I grant them protection and absolve them of all the sins they had committed in the early phase of their life. This I do instantly," Śrī Rāma expressed.

Hanumāna admired the words of his Lord. He hopped and went to Vibhīṣaṇa and admitted him into an audience of Śrī Rāma.

Vibhīṣaṇa viewed Śrī Rāma and Lakṣmaṇa with their hair tangled into a thick mass. Regaining his composure he lay prostrate at the feet of Śrī Rāma and presented himself as the younger brother of Rāvaṇa who had committed the sin of kidnapping Sītā jī, the epitome of the virtue of womanhood. He prayed for protection and absolving from the sins committed during this or the previous span of life.

He also said that he aspired only for the devotion to Śrī Rāma's feet and not for anything that the worldly life presents.

Śrī Rāma at once accepted Vibhīṣaṇa, awarded him with the kingship of Laṅkā. His formal coronation was celebrated in the presence of noteworthy monkey generals. Lakṣmaṇa brought the water from the sea in a jar for the purpose.

There was happiness all around. Hanumāna's happiness knew no bounds.

Rāvaṇa insulted and humiliated Vibhīṣaṇa. Compassionate Hanumāna showed him the way to the realm of Śrī Rāma Candra, who not only accepted him but also raised him to the status of the king of Laṅkā. He also admitted him to the inner circle of his dear ones. What is that which is not possible if Hanumāna jī vouchsafes the boons?

The Bridge

For three days Śrī Rāma prayed to the sea to allow him and his large army the passage to Laṅkā. But all in vain. Lastly he stringed his bow. When he vibrated the string, the world trembled, the mountain peaks tumbled and all quarters became dark. The seas and oceans became restless. The waves rose up and fell. There was turmoil in the entire creation. Śrī Rāma, the Lord of power and strength, was in deep anger.

The sea was overtaken by fear to its existence. He assumed the human form and appeared in person before Śrī Rāma. He begged for mercy. He apprised Śrī Rāma of two craftsmen or artisan monkeys in his army. Because of the blessings of sages they are capable of floating boulders on the sea. "They be deployed for constructing a bridge over my body," he said to Śrī Rāma. He also beseeched the Lord to take back his unfailing arrow or his existence would be in peril.

Śrī Rāma compassionately directed the arrow towards the land styled Drumakulya. It dried the watermass there and returned to his quiver.

As was suggested by the sea in human form, Śrī Rāma Candra commanded that the bridge across the see be constructed. Soon the monkeys and bears under the leadership of Hanumāna spread out to the areas far and away, uprooted the trees, lifted the boulders up, brought all these to the site and handed them down to Nala and Nila. They asked the worker monkeys to lay the material down on the surface of the sea. The bridge began taking shape. Hanumāna kept on inspiring the fellow monkeys who continued working with great gusto. Hanumāna was in the heart of every monkey. Monkey was in Hanumāna's heart.

The image of Sītā, languishing under the duress of captivity of Rāvaṇa, was in his heart. That image kept on motivating him to work and work, to dedicate every iota of his power and strength into the service of his Lord and he kept on motivating the fellow monkeys and bears into the service. The whole mass of dedicated beings worked ceaselesly for some days. The bridge took shape stage by stage. Soon the bridge got ready for the army of Śrī Rāma to traverse across the sea to the shore of Laṅkā.

Hanumāna's dedication, motivation and the selfless service reflected in the entire endeavour of bridge building. The Lord saw it, appreciated and gratefully acknowledged it in his heart. Each and every worker had become Hanumāna and Hanumāna was reflected in the heart of every worker.

Śrī Rāma and his army crossed the sea by the bridge and arrived at the other shore.

In the Battle Field

Next day, Śrī Rāma consulted his minister Jāmbavan. He was the wisest among all. On his advice Aṅgada was deputed to visit the court of Rāvaṇa as an emissary of Śrī Rāma. He carried a peace proposal. But, Rāvaṇa did not budge from his stand. As such war became imminent. The large scale devastation of the living beings and the material resources became inevitable. Both the armies were pitched against each other. The demonic forces were equipped with weapons of many varieties such as Bhindipāla, sword, three pronged spear, axe, Tomar, bow and arrow and mace. They were powerful and valorous, but as they had mastered some devilish methods, they could escape from defeat unseen or unnoticed. They could rain dust, water or blood and bone parts as a strategy of war. These methods could send the army of monkeys in turmoil and chaos but Śrī Rāma could end the devilish battle with one arrow. The monkeys and bears could then fight with renewed vigour and valour.

Rāma's army consisted of warriors such as Sugrīva, Vibhīṣaṇa, Aṅgada, Neela, Mainda, Dwivida, Gaja, Gavākśa, Gavaya, Sharabha, Gandhamādana, Panasa, Kumuda, Hara, Rambha, Jāmbavan, Suṣeṇa, Riṣabha, Durmukha and Shatabali. Besides these, there were lākhs of monkeys and bears. These had no weapons but their teeth, claws, fists, and slaps. They used these very judiciously. They would climb up the lofty buildings, break off their stones and rain them over the enemy establishments killing many without much strain. They would grind their strong teeth and would tear the cheeks open with their canines and incisors. They would tear off the enemy hearts open with their claws. They would dismember the arms off their bodies. Some monkeys and bears would catch hold of the enemy fighters and drown them in the seawaters or would burry them under the sands.

Śrī Hanumāna jī showed up as the God of death only. His presence sent tremors of fear up the bodies of enemy soldiers. He was fighting with boulders and rocks as weapons. He also used tree trunks and branches as weapons. He was not fighting in any fixed position. He was flying place to place meting out large scale ruin to the enemy forces. He was flying at a terrific speed and hitting at the enemy devastatingly. Each monkey soldier saw him beside himself and each demonic soldier encountered his face.

The well-known warriors of Rāvaṇa's ranks were demolished by Hanumāna jī. The news dislodged him from secured confidence. Meghanāda tried to assure him that he would go to the battle field in the chariot, which was equipped with unfailing weapons including the Brahmastra. Soon he was in the battle field.

He was aware of the striking power and speed of Hanumāna. Although he tried not to face him but how long could he escape from an encounter with him. But he wounded the star warriors of the Rāma army and succeeded in turning Rāma and Lakṣmaṇa also unconscious. Vibhīṣaṇa saw Jāmbavan wounded. He trembled at the sight. When he tried to give him some solace, he said that as his limbs were all pierced with arrows, he was unable to open his eyes and that he was recognising him through his voice only. He wanted to know if Hanumāna jī was safe and sound. He was worried about Sugriva and Aṅgada also.

Vibhīṣaṇa expressed his surprise at his lack of concern for Rāma and Lakṣmaṇa while he was showing all that concern for monkey warriors such as Hanumāna, Aṅgada and Sugrīva. He wanted to know the reason for that.

Jambavān replied that if one Hanumāna was safe and alive, the entire dead army of monkeys was alive. If Hanumāna was dead we all were dead though alive only bodily.

Instantly Hanumāna appeared there and touched his feet. Jambavān came to know by the feel of his touch that he was Hanumāna. He asked him to go and cover the whole monkey army as he alone from the monkey clan was endowed with wholesome valour. I do not consider anyone else suitable for that purpose. Rāma and Lakṣmaṇa regained consciousness in a short while.

Rāvaṇa decided to deploy Kumbhakarṇa at this turn of war. As soon as he appeared on the battle scene, the monkey and the bear soldiers started the torrent of boulders, rocks, tree trunks and branches aimed at him. But, he remained unmoved. This state sent up a wave of dismay in the rank and file of the Rāma's army. Inspired by some divine force, Hanumāna arrived at the scene. He wielded a blow of fist at his chest which felled him on the earth instantly. Then a single arrow of Śrī Rāma dealt him with deliverance.

Rāvaṇa was thus forced to enter the fray of battle. He was wielding a brilliant bow in his hand. The torment of arrows from his bow disarrayed the rank and file of the monkey formations. Hanumāna sprang into action and mounted his chariot in a fraction of a moment. Showing him his hand he cautioned him that, that hand would liberate the soul dwelling in the body he called as his and that he should not forget that he was the power which despatched the soul of Akṣa Kumāra to the other world. This infuriated Rāvaṇa gravely. He dealt a strong blow on to his chest. Hanumāna withstood that and returned an equally strong blow on to his chest. Rāvaṇa trembled and gave out that he deserved being his opponent in the battle.

Hanumāna denounced his striking power saying, "Damn it that you were still alive. Now you strike me once more. In reply to yours mine will dispatch you to the region of death."

The taunt of Hanumāna infuriated Rāvaṇa gravely. He dealt a severe blow of his fist on to the chest of Hanumāna which moved him only slightly. Regaining himself he found that Rāvaṇa had fallen upon Nīla, the commander of the monkey army. Hanuman slighted him saying that. "He would not fight him as he was entangled with another warrior of Rāma's army. If you free yourself of him I will see that your soul departs for the regions of the death."

Hanumāna's face was smeared with the blood of enemy soldiers. A glance at his face shook Rāvaṇa deeply.

Lakṣmaṇa came in front of Rāvaṇa who showered arrows at him, but could do no harm to him. Restless at his failure, he took up the famous weapon, Brahmāstra, and shot it at Lakṣmaṇa jī. The weapon tore the chest and entered it. Lakṣmaṇa fell unconscious. Rāvaṇa felt happy at it. He reached him and tried to move his body, but could not. He had lifted the mount Kailāśa but could not move Lakṣmaṇa jī.

At that very moment Hanumāna jī arrived at the site and dealt the severest blow of his fist on to Rāvaṇa's chest. He could not stand it. He fell down. Blood oozed out of his nose, eyes and ears. Trembling, shivering and quivering he came to the hind portion of his chariot, sat down and fell unconscious. His charioteer withdrew him from the battle field.

Hanumāna jī lifted Lakṣmaṇa jī and brought him where Rāma jī was at that hour. Laṣmaṇa recovered soon and regained consciouness.

Rāvaṇa returned to the battle field. He menaced the star warriors of Rāma army. Seeing this Rāmachandra jī attacked Rāvaṇa. Hanumāna jī saw that Rāvaṇa was on his chariot and Rāma was on foot. Hanumāna approached him and prayed that as Lord Viṣṇu, riding his vehicle Garuda wages war against the devils he should concede to ride his back and fight. Śrī Rāma consented to his request.

Rāma rode on the back of Hanumāna jī and gave a fight to Rāvaṇa. Lakṣmaṇa jī too rode on his back and fought the enemy. Hanumāna jī was thus playing a prominent role in the battle against Rāvaṇa. He became the sole reason for the deliverance of many devilish souls by way of bringing the departing ones into the presence of Śrī Rāma or doing them to death and remembering the name of his Lord while doing so.

The Sañjīwanī Episode

The battle was becoming fierce day by day. Meghanāda entered the fray of battle. He found Lakṣmaṇa facing him. He tormented the soldiers of Śrī Rāma with a ceaseless shower of sharp arrows. Lakṣmaṇa replied with powers. Hanumāna appeared with a large mountain on his shoulders and head and was about to drop it on the chariot of Meghanāda. He apprehended the design of Hanumāna jī and in order to save himself from being crushed under its heavy weight, he sprang up into the sky. Hanumāna jī challenged him time and again and he avoided the encounter with him, as that would prove fatal and decisive in the battle.

A fierce battle was fought between Lakṣmaṇa and Meghanāda. Lakṣmaṇa demolished his vehicle and killed his charioteer. Meghanāda had designs on his life but found himself helpless in face of Lakṣmaṇa's dexterity and power. Helpless, he shot the unfailing Brahama Śakti at him and that pierced into his broad chest. The blood gushed out of the wound and he fell unconscious. Meghanāda with his demon soldiers tried to lift him up but failed. He became too heavy for their combined strength.

The news of Lakṣmaṇa's falling to the missile of Meghanāda reached Hanumāna. He sprang up instantly and came to the place where Lakṣmaṇa was lying. The sight sent him into the frenzy of anger. He destroyed the entire strength of the devil soldiers present there.

Then he lifted the unconscious Lakṣmaṇa in his arms, took him where Rāma Candra was awaiting him. Viewing the weapon of Meghanāda piercing his chest, Śrī Rāma sank in the agony of apprehensive separation from his brother when he was still fighting a battle and roaming in exile.

Hanumāna came forward and consoled him. Addressing him, he said, "Lord, you need not worry till I am here. I can go to the heavens and bring ambrosia from there. I can squeeze this nectar out of the Moon and put it into the mouth of Lakṣmaṇa thus bringing down immortality to him. I can make a hole in the earth, reach the nether world through it, kill the nāgas and bring immortality drink from there and feed Lakṣmaṇa with it. Why this much only? I can destroy the Kāla himself, the killer of the entire living kingdom, and save him from death. Alongwith him all the living creatures would be free of the fear of death."

Hanumāna was exhibiting his annihilating tendency at that time. But Śrī Rāma Candra was to show the human tendencies. There Jāmbavān calmed Hanumāna jī down saying that he was capable of doing all that he was saying but dissuaded him from taking such a step and advised him to go to Lañkā town and bring the ablest physician, called Suṣeṇa from there. Hanumāna followed the word and without losing a moment lifted up the whole residential house of the physician, and put it down in the army camp. The speed, the motion and the jolts woke him up. When awakened, he came out and felt surprised at the sight of monkey soldiers around. Vibhīṣaṇa, whom the physician already knew well, explained to him the reason why he was brought there. Instantly he understood the situation and prescribed the administration of the herb Sañjīwanī which could be procured from a mount in the Himalayan range.

Suṣeṇa had become aware of the extraordinary powers of Hanumāna at the time of the Lankan inferno. He told Hanumāna that he alone could perform that feat and return with the herb before sunrise.

Hanumāna sprang up and took a giant stride towards the North. After a short while he visualised the Kailāś and Riṣabha mounts and the Dronagiri between them. The divine herbs were shining there. Before losing time in search for the right herb, he lifted up the whole mount off its foundation and sprang up to proceed towards Lañkā in the South.

On his onward journey to the Himālayas, he was presented with the obstacles by Kalanemi whom he did away with alongwith a nymph who was passing her days of curse in his company. She was Dhānyamalī by name.

On his return journey he flew over Ayodhyā. Bharata jī below mistook him for some devilish being, brought him down with an arrow. Falling down on the earth, he uttered the name of Śrī Rāma. Hearing the name of Śrī Rāma, Bharata regretted his mistake and offered his apologies.

Hanumāna narrated all the episodes of the story of Śrī Rāma. Bharata jī expressed his desire to accompany him to Lañkā. The sage Vaśiṣtha advised him not to leave Ayodhyā as that would amount to the breach of the word of his late father.

Hearing the news of Śrī Rāma, mothers gathered around him. They came to know of the events which had taken place during Rāma's exile into the forest. They also learnt about the duress Sīta jī had undergone in the captivity of Rāvaṇa and of the happenings in the battle.

Sumitrā told Hanumāna to convey to Rāma the message that he could return to Ayodhyā without Lakṣmaṇa but never without Sītā.

Kauśalyā contravening her word, conveyed that Rāma had left Ayodhya with Lakṣmaṇa and that he should return in no case without him.

Hanumāna was not prepared to lose time. He beseeched that he be allowed to leave for Lañkā without any loss of time as he must present himself before sunrise.

Bharata permitted; Hanumāna sprang up; reached Lanka, placed the mount at the feet of Śrī Rāma; Suṣeṇa administered the fragrance of the herb through the nasal passage. Lakṣmaṇa regained consciousness and sat up as if woken up from a slumber.

The whole episode sent Rāma into ecstasy. He took him in his arms and pressed him against his bosom.

Hanumāna was thinking that the Lord Himself was the doer of all that, while by His grace, he (Hanumāna) was being showered with all round praise.

Emancipation of Ahirāvaṇa

After recovering, Lakṣmaṇa challenged Meghanāda. A fierce battle between the two raged. Lastly Meghanāda's soul departed for its abode in the other world.

Rāvaṇa lost consciousness. On regaining it after a short while, he contemplated, "I have lost all my dependable warriors. Vibhīṣaṇa, whom I humiliated in the court publicly, is already with the enemy camp. My brave and mighty sons have been killed. The enemy is waging war from the foot hills of Trikūta. I am left alone. Whom to call up for help. Ahirāvaṇa, my friend in deed, would come to my rescue."

He propitiated Durgā to help him find the way to the nether world where Ahirāvaṇa dwelled. Ahirāvana appeared and offered his help, and enquired what the matter was and how he could be of any assistance.

Rāvaṇa narrated all the episodes leading to the finale which was imminent then. He apprised him of Rāma's battles with Khara and Dūṣaṇa which ensued as a consequence to the disfiguring of Śūrpanakhā, his sister. "Killing of Khara and Dūṣaṇa enraged me and I in a desguise of a mendicant stealthily kidnapped his beautiful wife Sītā. Rāma has been able to find the clue to the place of her captivity and is waging war at my door steps. I am fighting an almost lost war. Do what you can to save me, the remaining members of my family, my clan and the populace of Lañkā. Mine is almost a gone case. Rescue me if you can" forgetting his past achievements of valour and keeping away his egoistic look, Rāvaṇa spoke to him thus in a beseeching mode.

Ahirāvaṇa disapproved of his act of kidnapping. He said, "He would have appreciated a straight fight with Rāma to avenge the disfiguring of his sister and killing of Khara and

Dūṣaṇa. The act of kidnapping of a faithful wife like Sītā could not be condoned ethically, he opined. He also cautioned him that the destroyers of Khara, Dūṣaṇa, Kumbhakarna and Akṣaya and Meghanāda could not be ordinary human beings. "Still tell me plainly what you expect from me," Ahirāvaṇa enquired of him.

"You capture Rāma and Lakṣmaṇa anyhow and take them to your land and kill them there. These monkeys and bears will flee on their own," Rāvaṇa proposed to him.

Ahirāvaṇa consented. He also gave out that the light in the sky at midnight would signal the success of his plan.

It was near midnight. All the monkey and bear soldiers were tired and asleep. Hanumāna jī had extended his tail and taken the entire army in its circle. The tail circle was impregnable fort for the intruding enemy spies.

Ahirāvaṇa became apprehensive that he could not dare crossing into the tail fort. He changed his guise into that of Vibhīṣaṇa. As he was entering, Hanumāna jī enquired as to where he had been till that hour.

Ahirāvaṇa, in the guise of Vibhīṣaṇa, answered, "At the sea shore to perform evening prayer. Was delayed due to deep meditation in the name of Śrī Rāma."

This quietened Hanumāna jī.

Ahirāvaṇa entered the camp of Śrī Rāma stealthily. He perceived Śrī Rāma asleep. On his right was his great bow. On his left was Lakṣmaṇa. Rāma's hand was on the chest of Lakṣmaṇa. All the important warriors were asleep around Rāma and Lakṣmaṇa. Ahirāvaṇa had no courage to arouse them from slumber. He sent them into deep slumber with the help of sorcery. He lifted both the brothers quickly, came out of the camp, sprang up into the sky and sped towards his palace. He succeeded in keeping his word that he had given to Rāvaṇa.

Suddenly a streak of light shone up in the sky, Rāvaṇa became exceedingly happy over the successful execution of the plan.

Now Hanumāna jī was his target.

By the sudden shine of the streak of light, Vibhīṣaṇa woke up. Not finding Śrī Rāma jī and Lakṣmaṇa in the camp, he shrieked. A sharp furore spread up over the army establishment.

All warriors of Rāma's camp were taken aback. No one could think that someone could steal into the camp while Hanumāna jī was on guard. Hanumāna also could not resolve the puzzle.

Vibhīṣaṇa said, "no one could steal and no one did in the dead of the night." Hanumāna retorted, "you did return late at night from the shore. I encountered you."

Vibhīṣaṇa came out with the explanation, "I was at the feet of the Lord since evening. I had not even gone to the sea shore. I made it known to all including Hanumāna jī; Hanumāna declared that he would search both of them out, be they in the nether world or in the world above, and that he was capable of destroying the time itself in order to find out Śrī Rāma and Lakṣmaṇa.

In a moment Vibhīṣaṇa resolved the puzzling saying that only one person could wear on his guise and that was Ahirāvaṇa. He cautioned Hanumāna jī carefully to find him in the nether regions which, Ahirāvaṇa of the demonic clan, ruled over. Vibhīṣaṇa took his leave at once for the place of Ahirāvaṇa. He equipped him with all necessary information about the routes, entry and defence systems of his township.

In a moment Hanumāna jī was at the gate of the town of Ahirāvaṇa. There he was encountered by a fierce monkey guard who gave out his name as Makaradhwaja and said that he was the son of Hanumāna. Hanumāna became curious about the truth of the statement as he was a staunch celibate.

Makradhwaja satisfied his curiosity but did not allow him to enter the temple of Goddess where Ahirāvaṇa was preparing to sacrifice both the brothers and offer them to the Goddess.

Hanumāna jī hit him strongly with his fist and on his being unconscious for a while, tied him with his own tail and entered the temple swiftly.

Hanumāna jī saw the meticulous preparation for the rite of sacrifice and both the brothers in bondage.

Hanumāna jī reached the back of the idol and touched it. The idol sank into the depth. Hanumāna jī stood in the place thus created. He assumed a fierce form with the mouth wide open.

Ahirāvana performed the worship. When he offered oblation, Hanumāna jī, who was acting as the Goddess, swallowed it. This pleased Ahirāvaṇa immensely. He thought that the Goddess was extremely pleased that day as she accepted the oblation personally.

Ahirāvaṇa called for sweets and other preparations from the kitchen of the palace in large quantities. Hanumāna jī devoured the entire quantity without much strain or effort. The devil took it for the pleasure of the Goddess.

Lastly he got both the brothers summoned for the sacrificial rite. Both were brought. They were bathed, attired, decorated and worshipped. Soon he declared, that they were going to be offered to the Goddess as oblation.

Lakṣmaṇa was bewildered at no action mode of Śrī Rāma. He sought his permission and tried to know what he should do. Śrī Rāma replied that when in peril people remembered him. When they were in peril they should remember Hanumāna jī.

Lakṣmaṇa wanted to know whether Hanumāna was there. Śrī Rāma lifted his eyelid and Hanumāna roared from the seat of the Goddess. He jumped on to Ahirāvaṇa. His eyes closed out of fear. Hanumāna snatched the sword from his hand in one jolt. Ahirāvaṇa took up the second sword and struck it at the body of Hanumāna jī. It broke into pieces. Hanumāna now severed his head in one stroke. His body and head fell in the fire which he had prepared for Rāma and Lakṣmaṇa. The fire burnt him down to ashes.

Hanumāna did to death the demonic guards present there. He seated Rāma and Lakṣmaṇa on his shoulders and set out on his journey to the upper regions, leaving the nether world below.

At the gate of the town he introduced his son Makaradhwaja while freeing him of the bondage of his own tail. He also made it known to his Lord how the son was born to him and by whom. Śrī Rāma jī enthroned him as the king of the nether world.

Hanumāna jī applied the mark on his forehead and advised him to follow the path of virtue and to remember the name of the Lord always and in every circumstance. Makaradhwaja touched the feet of the Lord, Lakṣmaṇa, and his father and they left soon after.

As soon as the trio touched the land of Lañkā, the tumult of the exclamation of joy rose high rending all the regions and quarters.

The face of Rāvaṇa blackened at the magnitude of the tumult.

At the Feet of the Mother

Rāvaṇa was destined to die at the hands of Śrī Rāma Candra. He fought very bravely but could not escape defeat and death. One last arrow of Śrī Rāma jī pierced his navel and he fell and died.

Vibhīṣaṇa cried at the sight.

His wives gathered around his dead body and wailed ceaselessly. Śrī Rāma ordered Lakṣmaṇa to solace the crying and wailing men and women of the Rāvaṇa family.

Lakṣmaṇa carried out the instructions to his best capacity.

Vibhīṣaṇa became quiet after some time. Śrī Rāma told him to perform the last rites of his elder brother which he did with all respect and care.

Then, by the orders of his elder brother Lakṣmaṇa, with the help of and in the company of Sugrīva, Aṅgada, Jambavān and Hanumāna enthroned Vibhīṣaṇa as the king of Lañkā. Holy water was procured in gold jars and was sprinkled on his head to the chanting of Vedic hymns.

Vibhīṣaṇa, followed by the celebrities of Lañkā carrying precious gifts, presented himself for an audience with Śrī Rāma. He lay prostrate at his feet.

Śrī Rāma Candra beheld the giant Hanumāna standing in his presence. He asked him to enter Lañkā and convey to Sīta the news of the death of Rāvaṇa, and also to apprise her of the well being of Lakṣmaṇa and warriors such as Aṅgaḍa, Sugrīva and Jambavan.

Hanumāna roared in ecstasy. There could be no happier news than this for him to convey to Sīta jī. Hanumāna proceeded for the Aśoka Vāṭikā. He was already familiar with roads to the woods. He was walking joyously hopping and dancing, and was being accorded a hearty ovation at every nook and corner of the roads by the people.

By the orders of Vibhīṣaṇa the well-known soldiers were escorting Hanumāna. Soon he arrived at the woods of the Aśoka Vāṭikā. Sītā jī was sitting under the same tree under which he had seen her earlier. The demonic women were sitting around her. Swiftly Hanumāna ran towards her and lay prostrate at her feet. After a while he broke the news that war with Rāvaṇa was over. Śrī Rāma jī had come out victorious and Rāvaṇa was dead. His army was vanquished. Vibhīṣaṇa had been enthroned as the king of Lañkā. Śrī Rāma jī and all his lieutenants in the war were safe and sound and so were the monkey and bear soldiers.

Out of ecstasy, Sītā jī could not utter a syllable for some time. After a while she spoke, "Nothing in the three worlds could give me that happiness as this news has. You have done a great service to me. I do not know how to reward you. I can never repay the debt that I owe to you."

Hanumāna humbly replied that a son can never be free of the debt that he owes to his mother. "Mother! I am at your feet, I yearn earnestly to be at your feet and serve my Lord Śrī Rāma jī and you. I have no other desire to fulfil," Hanumāna spoke humbly.

Sītā jī, hearing the soft and noble speech of Hanumāna, said, "The language you speak is ennobled by such qualities as decency and propriety. You are the capable son of the God of Wind. You embody the qualities of virtue and piety. All niceties have converged in your character. I bless you that all nobilities may be enshrined in your heart and that you may always enjoy the favour of Śrī Rāma and Lakṣmaṇa."

Hanumāna got angry with devilish women who were always the source of fear and anxiety for Sītā jī. She quietened him saying, "what they were doing was due to the commands of Rāvaṇa. Now as he is no more their attitude has calmed. They are now humble and polite. They deserve our mercy and compassion."

Begging to leave, he requested for some message. Expressing her gratitude to Śrī Hanumāna, she said that she was keen on being at the feet of her Lord as soon as possible.

Śrī Rāmeśwaram and the Lord of Hanumāna

With the emancipation of Rāvaṇa the mission Lañkā was over. As a finale, Vibhīṣaṇa was enthroned and crowned the king of Lañkā. Now Śrī Rāmachandra jī in the company of Lakṣmaṇa and Sītā, with the entourage consisting of Hanumāna, Sugrīva, Añgada and Jāmbavan and escorted by many monkeys and bears, mounted the vehicle Puṣpaka It proceeded by the sky route.

Puṣpaka landed at the mount Gandha Madana. There Sītā jī went through the test fire. There sage Agastya and many ascetics from the forest Daṇḍaka were present at the purification rite. The sages offered obeisance to Śrī Rāma and Sītā jī.

Śrī Rāma Candra bowed humbly at the feet of the sages and expressed his remorse at the annhilation of the whole clan of the sage Pulastya, the great Brāhmana. I want to absolve myself of the sin which ensues the act of Brāhmanicide or the killing of a Brāhmana or Brāhmanas, said Śrī Rāma Candra.

The expression pleased the sages who wanted to condone the act saying that, that was done for reaffirming the path of Dharma, Virtue and destroying the regime of the sin. They further said that he, Rāma, was Dharma incarnate; no sin could shear him. "Still", they continued, "in order to set a tradition he should found a seat for Lord Śiva; The Śiva–Liñga, as founded by him, would be known by the name Rāmeśwaram among the populace and in the progeny of the future. This would absolve him of the sin as well as grant deliverance to the lay men and women approaching there for worshipping.

The auspicious time for the initiation and completion of the ceremony was passing. An icon of Śivaliñga should be quickly procured from mount Kailāśa and installed here. Hanumāna may, therefore, be dispatched soon to mount Kailāśa. Śrī Rāma asked him for the job and he flew with the speed of the wind and in no time reached Kailāśa. There he propitiated Lord Śiva and obtained from him the icon. Instantly he proceeded southward with the speed of electricity. As the time was passing and Hanumāna was not to be seen, the learned sages suggested the Śivaliñga made by Sītā jī out of the sands may be installed. As the sages ordained, Rāma began chanting the hymns and installed the icon of sands made by Sītā jī on the mount of Gandhamadana in the vicinity of the bridge. Instantly Lord Śiva and this spouse Pāravatī appeared in the icon. The viewing of the icon by the people will destroy the heaps of the sins in a moment, Lord Śiva vouchsafed.

The Lord and Pāravatī disappeared after the moment. Hanumāna arrived late. Seeing that the ceremony was over, he felt morose. He said, "I reached Kailāśa in no time. I could not lay my hand on an icon resembling Lord Śiva. In order to propitiate him and to obtain from Him the icon, I practised severe penance for some time. Then the Lord vouchsafed me with this icon in my hand. What to do of it?"

Seeing him disheartened, Rāma consoled him saying that, "if you are able to perceive the truth you will realise that what you do is in fact my doing and what I do is in reality your doing. Thus you have installed this icon of Lord Śiva which, you think, I have."

Śrī Rāma further said, "Today is a very auspicious day. You install this icon which is in your hand. This icon, the Śivaliñga, will be known in the three worlds by your name, the Lord of Hanumāna. First the devotees will view the icon installed by you and then they would come to have a view of the Liñga installed by me. You were also the instrument of killing of innumerable Brāhmana demons. Although the sin cannot smear your soul, still killing of a Brāhmana cannot be styled an act of virtue, whatsoever might be the cause. So by installing this icon by your hand, which you have brought all the way from Kailāśa, you will be absolved of all the sins committed knowingly or unknowingly."

Hanumāna lay prostrate at the feet of his Lord Śrī Rāma. He prayed to him and he prayed to Sītā jī.

Later, following the word of Śrī Rāma, he installed the Lliñga towards the North of the Liñgam installed by Śrī Rāma.

Śrī Rāma ordained that whoever worshipped Śrī Rāmeśwar without worshipping Hanumanīśwaram would worship Rāmeśwaram in vain.

Hanumāna accordingly installed the Śivaliñgam towards the North of the Setu Bandha Rāmeśwaram.

Śrī Rāma Meets Añjanā

The Pushpak was detailed into the service of Śrī Rāma by Vibhīṣaṇa, now the king of Lañkā. Śrī Rāma made Hanumāna, Sugrīva, Añgada and Jāmbavan and some monkey and bear soldiers mount the craft. Śrī Rāma was very keen to return to Ayodhyā and meet his brother Bharata before the time limit expired. The craft flew past all the notable points of the events connected with the story. Śrī Rāma showed all those points on the land and narrated the events which took place there after Sītā jī had parted from him. He showed to her the place where Rāvaṇa had fallen. The Setu Bandha and all other places connected with episodes.

Soon the craft flew over Kiṣkindhā. Śrī Rāma commanded the craft to land there. The ladies of palace accompanying Tāra, came to meet Sītā jī. Sītā jī expressed her desire that the ladies also join the coronation ceremony of Śrī Rāma jī in Ayodhyā. Śrī Rāma consented and the ladies made up their mind to mount the craft on its way to Ayodhyā.

Hanumāna expressed his longing to present himself in audience of his revered mother Añjanā. Śrī Rāma agreed; the craft took to the route to the Kañcana Giri where Añjanā lived. With Śrī Rāma and Hanumāna, all alighted. The large entourage consisting of the wives of Vibhīṣaṇa, the wives of the monkey warriors, Lakṣmaṇa, Aṅgada and the large number of monkey and bear soldiers proceeded to present themselves in her audience.

Seeing her, Hanumāna ran up to meet her. She took him into her arms and pressed him against her bosom. Hanumāna's voice choked. Hardly he could utter 'ma'. Añjanā was meeting her son after a long time. She pressed him from the core of her heart.

Hanumāna introduced all the ladies present there to his mother. He also introduced Śrī Rāma and Lakṣmaṇa. Añjanā was going to fall at his feet when Śrī Rāma mentioning the name of his father saluted her and requested her to sit beside him. The ladies and the large number of monkeys and bears lay prostrate at her feet.

Añjanā taking the soft hands of Śrī Rāma in her hands expressed the sentiment of being a true and fulfilled mother as her son was in his service and had performed miraculous feats of valour and bravery.

Hanumāna narrated all the episodes of the story to his mother. She felt somewhat disgusted and said, "Why and how you did not break the mount Trikūta open off its foundation and submerge that in the waters of the ocean along with the fort of Lañkā and its inhabitants? Why Śrī Rāma Candra, Lakṣmaṇa had to fight and all these monkeys and bears were deployed into the battle, Why? Of what use and service were you?.

Hanumāna replied, "mother! I could do all this and much more than that but Shri Jāmabvān had detailed me only to find out the clue to Sītā jī's place and convey the detailed information to Śrī Rāma. So I acted accordingly."

Censuring Hanumāna jī for his deeds having fallen short of her expectations Añjanā denounced her son blatantly.

Lakṣmaṇa by his looks disapproved of her statement. Añjanā guessed it.

She took out her one breast, drew milk out of it and sprinkled it at a peak nearby. The peak fell apart into two. Lakṣmaṇa's disbelief about the strength and impact of Añjanā's milk proved baseless. Añjanā reiterated the power of her milk and stated that Hanumāna was nourished with that milk and that could never prove contrary to her expectations.

The entourage bowed at her feet and besought her permission to leave. Añjanā consented and the craft carrying the crowd took off for Ayodhyā.

Breaking the Happy News

The Puṣpaka craft flew over Prayāgarāja, Ayodhyā was visible from there. Rāmachandra was moved with the sentiment of nostalgia.

He willed and the craft landed on the bank Triveni; Sītā jī and others bathed in the holy confluence there. They invited the learned Brāhmanas and satisfied them with gifts.

Śrī Rāma Candra called Hanumāna and detailed him about the future plans. He said to him, "Go fast and return with the news of the welfare of all the people of Ayodhyā."

At Śringaverapura, you will meet Niṣāda Rāja. Tell him that we are safe. He will give you the news about Bharata; from there you go to Ayodhyā. "At Ayodhyā you ask about the welfare of the people. Also tell Bharata and others that we are safe and returning to Ayodhyā having completed the period of exile as was desired by our late father."

"Also observe closely the facial expression of Bharata. If you find that he has any desire for the kingdom, then let me know. I will let him enjoy the pleasures of life as a king and I will go elsewhere to live the life of an ascetic. In every respect I desire for Bharata's happiness. Meet him and return soon," Śrī Rāma detailed Hanumāna for the advance.

Hanumāna put on the guise of a Brāhmana, touched the feet of Śrī Rāma and proceeded for Ayodhyā with the speed of Garuda.

At Śringaverapura he met Niṣāda Rāja. There he broke the news of the safe returning of Śrī Rāma, Lakṣmaṇa and Sītā jī. He also informed him about the large entourage journeying with them. The joy of Niṣāda Rāja knew no bounds. He began preparing for a rising ovation to welcome him.

On the way he visited Parashurāma Tīrtha. Proceeding further, beyond river Gomatī he saw the hermitage of Śrī Bharata jī at a distance of one *kosa* from Ayodhyā. He was gloomy and humourless. He gave up the luxury of kingly life. He lived as an ascetic at Nandigrāma. He would worship the wooden footwears of Śrī Rāma daily and conducted the state business as a servant of Śrī Rāma. At Nandigrāma he followed the life style as he thought Śrī Rāma was following in the forests. He used to put on the saffron robes. As was he, so were his ministers, generals and the priests.

Hanumāna saw that Bharata had become very weak. He would not take full meals. Most of the time he remembered Śrī Rāma, Lakṣmaṇa and Sītā and shed tears ceaselessly. He spent fourteen years in the agony of separation. He counted each day and looked for the arrival of Śrī Rāma. Now only one day was left. He lost all patience in wait which was to come to an end ultimately. He had deployed the state cavalry upto Śringaverapura with the view that as soon as Śrī Rāma arrived at the bank of Gaṅgā, the news would be relayed to him without losing much time.

There was rancor in his heart that he was the cause of so much suffering to Śrī Rāma, Lakṣmaṇa and Sītā. He made them roam the forests which were bereft of the necessary comforts of living. He was sitting in front of the footwears of Śrī Rāma jī and lamenting the separation and his living in exile when Hanumāna appeared and broke the news that Rāma was returning home on the expiry of the period of exile. He had killed Rāvaṇa and finished his kingdom except Vibhīṣana. Lakṣmaṇa and Sītā were safe and were coming with him.

Bharata received the news with excitement of utmost degree and enquired of his identity as he was putting on the guise of a Brāhmana.

Hanumāna disclosed, "I am the messenger of Śrī Rāma. I am Hanumāna, the son of the God of Wind. Śrī Rāma detailed me to know about your well being and to convey to you that He, with Lakṣmaṇa and Sītā, was coming and was well."

Bharata took Hanumāna in his arms and embraced him. Bharata asked him to tell him all about him. Hanumāna narrated all events related with the battle in Laṅkā, killing of Rāvaṇa, victory of Śrī Rāma and recovering Sītā from his captivity.

He wanted to know whether Śrī Rāma ever remembered him.

Hanumāna sought his permission to leave and reach Śrī Rāma. Bharata permitted and he at once set off.

In the meantime Śrī Rāma reached the hermitage of the sage Bharadwāja. He bowed at the feet of the sage. So did all. The sage blessed Śrī Rāma and all who were with him.

Śrī Rāma enquired of him about Bharata. The sage greeted and praised him for demolishing the stronghold of the demons. He further said, "you already know everything. Still since you asked me, I tell you that every thing is well with Bharata and Ayodhyā though Bharata has become very weak."

The sage offered him hospitality, which he accepted. Soon Hanumāna arrived with the news of Bharata and Ayodhyā. Hanumāna's account of Bharata confirmed the description of Bharata as the sage had given.

Without losing time Śrī Rāma and the entourage boarded the craft and left for Ayodhyā.

At Ayodhyā, soon after Hanumāna jī had left, Bharata gave the news of Śrī Rāma coming home to Śrī Guru Vaśiṣṭha and the mothers. They all felt joyous. A wave of excitement ran through Ayodhyā. All men, women, young and old alongwith children and babies in arms came running out of their homes to have a view of Rāma, Lakṣmaṇa and Sītā jī after fourteen long years. The big crowd gathered and moved to accord a tumultuous ovation to Śrī Rāma, Lakṣmaṇa and Sītā. They danced and sang in excitement of the utmost degree. There was joy in the hearts which knew no bounds. There was none who was not out in happiness.

The chariots, the riders, and foot soldiers in ten thousand each waited to welcome Śrī Rāma, Lakṣmaṇa and Sītā at the entrance to the town. The milling crowd sent up a roar of joy when the craft Puṣpaka hovered over and then landed. Śrī Rāma alighted. Sītā followed and then Lakṣmaṇa came out. The ladies of Lañkā and Kiṣkindhā followed. Then came Sugrīva, Aṅgada, Hanumāna, Jāmbavān and many others. Rāma instructed Puṣhpaka to return to Kubera.

The tumult that rose up rent the air and reverberated the regions of the sky and the earth.

Śrī Rāma beheld Vaśiṣṭha, Vāmadeva and the holy sages in front, he laid his weapon on the earth and ran up to touch their feet. Lakṣmaṇa followed. Vaśiṣṭha lifted Rāma up and pressed him against his chest and blessed. Śrī Rāma bowed to the Brāhmanas and received their blessings.

Bharata, Śatrughna and the mothers watched. Bharata carried the footwears of Śrī Rāma on his head. Taking them down, he placed them in front of him. He held his feet. The eyes of Śrī Rāma and Bharata were brimming with tears. Rāma lifted Bharata up to his bosom but he would not leave his feet. With an effort only he could lift him up.

Rāma enquired of him how he was and how he passed the period of his exile. Bharata only said that he was saved only by his compassion. Now all was well that he was there.

Śrī Rāma then embraced Śatrughna Bharata and Lakṣmaṇa.

On one side were Sugrīva, the king of monkey clan, his wives, prince Aṅgada, Vibhīṣaṇa, the king of Lañkā, his wives, Jāmbavan, Maya and, Dwivida, Nala and Neela and the crowd of monkeys and bears and on the other were Vaśiṣṭha, the mothers Kauśalyā, Sumitrā and Kaikeyī accompanied by the other ladies of the Royal family. Between these the meeting of the brothers took place.

The mothers lifted up Sītā falling at their feet and washing them with tears one after another.

Thus was enacted the finale of the story that begun fourteen years back.

The Epitome of Great Devotion

Śrī Rāma ascended the throne of Ayodhyā. Sītā occupied the place beside him. The mother earth was exuberant. The wind was soft and cheerful. The Gods were jubiliant. They showered the celestial flowers on Śrī Rāma and Sītā jī.

Śrī Rāma bestowed large gifts on the sages and Brāhmaṇas. Pleased and happy, they blessed Him and Sītā Jī.

Śrī Rāma then gifted the king of Kiṣkindha, his friend Sugrīva, with gold necklaces studded with the gems of the divine lustre. He gave Aṅgada a pair of armlets, which wẹre studded with the blue sapphires. Likewise Vibhīṣaṇa, Jāmbavān, Dwivida, Maya, and, Nala and Neela were decorated with gifts and honours.

He also presented Sīta jī with clothes and ornaments of various descriptions. Once the God of Wind had decorated Śrī Rāma Candra with a valuable necklace of pearls of celestial beauty and lustre. He adorned Sītā jī with that ornament.

Sītā jī observed that Śrī Rāma had honoured his war companion with various decorations but had omitted Hanumāna till then. Sītā jī looked towards Śrī Rāma and expressed her desire to honour him. Śrī Rāma permitting, she gave away that string of shining pearls to Hanumāna. With that string round his neck he looked extremely charming. The gathering applauded the event and the gift. All acknowledged that he was endowed with the rare qualities such as brilliance, courage, valour, prowess, power, calibre, humility and wisdom par excellence. They all felt that Hanumāna fully deserved the gift.

But Hanumāna felt differently. He wanted to see if the pearls reflected the image of his master. He started plucking pearl after pearl and crushing it under his molars to see if the inside showed the image he was looking for. But there was none of that nature. Ultimately he destroyed the entire ornament.

Vibhīṣaṇa, Aṅgada, Sugrīva and all other disapproved of this behaviour on his part. The courtiers could not hold back their comments. They muttered that he was after all a monkey.

Vibhīṣaṇa ultimately questioned as to the reason behind the destruction of such an ornament, each pearl of which could equal an empire.

Hanumāna retorted that he was looking for the reflection of the image of his master in each of the pearls but they were not of that type. So he discarded them all.

The reply angered Vibhīṣaṇa further. He sarcastically remarked that if these pearls did not reflect the image of his master, his physique would, which resembled a mount.

Hanumāna affirmed that it did so. If not, he would do away with that. It had no use for him. He asked them to see for themselves if they did not believe his words. Instantly he placed both his hands on his chest and with the sharp nails tore it apart. And lo! Rāma jī with Sītā jī were beheld sitting on the throne in the open chest of Hanumāna.

The gathering was taken aback. The inside and outside of Śrī Hanumāna were permeated with the spirit of Śrī Rāma. What to say of Sītā and Rāma, Bharata, Śatrughna, Lakṣmaṇa, Kauśalya and the other mothers all were dear to him more than his own life.

Sugrīva left for Kiṣhkindhā. Before leaving he deputed Hanumāna in the service of Śrī Rāma.

Aṅgada begged that he may he remembered to Śrī Rāma every now and then. Hanumāna was the closest to Śrī Rāma.

When Bharata, Śatrughana and Lakṣmaṇa intended to speak to Śrī Rāma, they looked towards Hanumāna. Śrī Rāma knows every thing. Still, he asks Hanumāna as to what the matter is, Śrī Hanumāna jī apprises the master of the desire of his brother or brothers to petition about something to him. Śrī Rāma nods and he presents.

Śrī Rāma is in Hanumāna and he in Rāma. When he consummated his playful acts on this plane of life, before leaving for his abode, he ordained Hanumāna to stay and live on the earth till his story prevailed there.

Hanumāna jī instantly accepted the command and promised to the Lord that he would live on this planet till the story of his playful divine acts prevailed there.

Lord Śankara once acknowledged to his spouse, Pāravatī, that none was more fortunate and devoted to the feet of Śrī Rāma than Hanumāna whom Śrī Rāma himself dearly adored.

Truth is that if Hanumāna favours somebody with his grace he is fulfilled forever.

Childlike Simplicity

In the presence of Sīta jī Hanumāna behaves as a child does in presence his mother.

Once he was feeling hungry, went to Sīta jī and asked for something to eat. Sīta jī replied that she would give him a *Modaka,* a ball-shaped sweet, made of gram flour, sugar and pure ghee after she had taken bath. Hanumāna sat near the threshold of her room, waiting for her to come out of the bathroom.

After bath she began doing her hair. Having done her hair, she drew a streak of vermillion in the parting of her hair. Hanumāna became curious about the use of vermillion.

Sīta jī told him that the streak of vermillion in the parting of a lady's hair signified the prayer for long life of her husband.

Hanumāna was all for the long life of Śrī Rāma jī. His thought process started functioning. If a streak of vermillion signified the prayer for long life of a lady's husband, heap of it would mean prayer for eternity of life of his master.

So, Hanumāna applied oil all over his person and smeared it with vermillion. In this excercise, he forgot all about his hunger.

Thus smeared all over his body, Hanumāna jī reached the court of Śrī Rāma. Seeing him in that guise, some smiled and many laughed. Even Śrī Rāma could not restrain his curiosity. He asked him about the reason for all that.

Hanumāna, his hands folded in humble prayer, replied, "Master! Mother Jānakī applies a streak of vermillion in the parting of her hair for your long life; I applied all over my body for eternity of your life."

Śrī Rāma declared, "Today is Tuesday, whosoever will apply oil and vermillion on the body of Śrī Hanumāna jī, all his wishes will be granted."

There are many other anecdotes about Hanumāna's childlike simplicity and devotion to Śrī Rāma Candra. They are narrated by the story tellers and preachers of Śrī Rāma sect. All show that the devotion of Śrī Hanumāna towards his duty was supreme and par exellence.

Wherever the people would worship Śrī Rāma or repeat his name or sing devotional songs dedicated to him, Hanumāna would be present there instantly. And also, wherever Hanumāna is worshipped or sung, Śrī Rāma would be instantly present to vouchsafe the devotees.

Truly speaking, Hanumāna is Rāma and Rāma Hanumāna in the final reckoning. Rāma is the principle, Hanumāna is its force and application.

The Supreme Truth

Once Rāma and Sītā were sitting in the presence of the great Yogi Maharshi Vaśiṣtha and listening to his exposition of philosophy.

Hanumāna's eyes were riveted on to the face of Śrī Rama who noticed and realised the profundity of his attention. He drew the attention of Sīta jī and told her that Hanumāna was the embodiment of the selfless service. His devotion was unwavering and undivided. He truly deserved the imparting of the supreme wisdom.

Sīta jī, addressing him, said, "Śrī Rāma is the supreme consciousness. He is beyond the purview of attributes; sure and unmixed consciousness; beyond permutation and change; never changing pure existence beyond the range of ever changing phenomena; omnipresent, omniscient and self referral supreme being he is."

"Know me as the entity causing all creation, sustenance and disintegration. Never tiring of my involvement, I remain all the time busy with these creative activities. The ignorant transfer all these phenomena on to Rāma. He is in fact an entity beyond all entities. He is without attributes, still the source of all attributes. He is formless, still the originator of all the forms. I am his instrument. Through me he operates though in overall consideration he does not operate. There are Guṇas, there is prakṛti, Guṇas act and react on Guṇas. Thus the chain action starts. He, Rāma, only witnesses all changes generated by my power."

"Śrī Rāma neither walks nor stays, neither grieves, nor desires; neither accepts nor shuns. He is changeless and generates no result or consequences. Due to the illusory nature of Māyā, He appears as the ignorant view him.

Then Śrī Rāma revealed his heart to him, "If you look at a pond of water, you will see three types of the sky (1) Mahākāśa, the space that wraps all things, persons, beasts and entities – gigantic and minuscules, (2) The other is confined within the bounds of the pond, and (3) The reflection. Similarly the consciousness too is of three types: (1) That which is surmounted by the intellect, (2) That which is complete in every respect, and (3) That which reflects in the intellect. The third one is that which signifies the apparent consciousness. This is the doer of activities. But the ignorant transfer the attributes of creativity on the Atman which is beyond all attributes and creativity. The apparent consciousness is the bounded consciousness. In actuality, the apparent consciousness and the real consciousness beyond all appearances, is one and the same. Tattvamasi states beyond doubt that all dualities, real or apparent, are one and the same."

"This knowledge should never be imparted to the mean and the crook."

Aśwamedha

The sage Agastya inspired Śrī Rāma to perform a Yajña in which a horse was to be sacrificed. The sage Vaśiṣtha selected the horse. It was very strong. Its mouth was red, it was pure white, its ears were black, it was very beautiful. It was adorned properly. Sandal paste was applied on its forehead. A garland was tied round its neck. On its head a gold plate was tied. An inscription on it ran as under – Whosoever thinks himself stronger than Śrī Rāma Candra, the king of kings, may hold this horse up, to be forcefully released by our armies later. In such a case, the monarch who dares to hold the horse up should be prepared to give us a fight. If he suffers defeat at our hands he should he prepared to submit to our sovereignty.

Śrī Rāma made Śatrughna responsible for the horse's safety. Addressing Hanumāna, Śrī Rāma expressed his gratitude in these words, "Great valorous Hanumāna! I have obtained this undisputed vast kingdom due to your bravery and sacrifice. Though humans, we crossed the ocean. You became instrumental in my reunion with my beloved wife Sītā. All this became possible due to your strength and courage. I command you also to go with the horse as its guard."

"You protect my younger brother Śatrughna, as you protected me. If he goes astray, do bring him round onto the right path."

Hanumāna felt exalted.

The commander of the force was Kālajit. Puṣkala, the son of Bharata, also accompanied.

Prominent ministers, who were learned and wise, accompanied the force. All were joyous and full of courage.

The army crossed the river Payoṣṇī. Hanumāna and the entire entourage visited all the hermitages on the way. The monkeys and bears were following as soldiers. The army consisted of all the four wings.

The army and its leaders reached the hermitage of the sage Cyavana, the son of the sage Bhrigu. The hermitage was inhabited by the sages who had shed away their natural and instinctive hostility.

The sage Cyavana felt exalted by the visit of Hanumāna and Śatrughna and prayed aloud, "Save me from the vices O, Rāma and from the binding impact of desire and karma. Bless me O Lord! With the dust of your feet."

Cyavana got prepared to walk down to Ayodhya to meet Śrī Rāma and bow at his feet. Śatrughna invited him to grace the sacrificial ceremony. Hanumāna offered to reach the sage and his family to Ayodhyā. Śatrughna allowed and Hanumāna carried him and his family to Ayodhyā on his back and reached there without losing much time. Soon he returned to rejoin the army.

The army then reached the town Cakrāṅkā. It was ruled over by the monarch Subāhu who was, being a great ruler, also a great devotee of Lord Viṣṇu.

His son Damana was out on a game in the forest. He sighted the horse and caught it. Damana was a great warrior. He surprised the army of Śatrughna by his valour, courage and fighting skill. A large number of soldiers of the army were lost, but Damana fell unconscious.

Then Subāhu came out. His younger brother Suketu joined the battle. His sons Citṛāṅga and Vicitra also joined. He reorganised his fighting forces in the formation styled Krauñca. The wings, the bill and tail were occupied by the warriors of calibre.

A fierce battle ensued. The son of Bharata, Puṣkala, severed the head of Citrāṅga. The remaining warriors raged a still more fierce battle. Hanumāna hit at Subāhu's chest with his foot. Subāhu could not withstand it. He fell and vomitted blood. In the state of unconsciousness he saw a vision. Śrī Rāma was performing a yajña; Brahmā was chanting the hymns of the Vedas. The great Brāhmanas were offering oblation to Gods through the Fire God.

Subāhu regained consciousness. Instantly he asked his brother and sons to end the battle. He started narrating his dream like experience. He said, "In the days gone by I had gone to the sacred places in search for real wisdom. I reached the hermitage of the sage Asitāṅga. He explained to me that Śrī Rāma was Brahman himself and Sītā jī his power. I started arguing against his views. He got angry and cursed me, "You shall never be able to achieve wisdom of true knowledge." I held his feet and begged his pardon. He pardoned and said "When you catch the sacrificial horse of Śrī Rāma, Hanumāna would hit at your chest and you will gain the wisdom of true knowledge."

"Today is that day when we are all fulfilled. The wisdom has dawned upon me." Subāhu presented a large number of elephants, horses, heaps of precious gems, pearls and many gold ornaments to Śatrughna. Also, he expressed regrets for Damana having waged the battle with the army of Śrī Rāma under the command of Śatrughna and protected by Hanumāna. Subāhu fell at the feet of Hanumāna when he saw him. So did his brother and sons. Śatrughna took them in his arms one by one and embraced.

The army advanced further and reached the bank of Narmadā. The sage Āraṇyaka lived in a hut made of leaves of Palāśa, there. Āraṇyaka was a devotee of Śrī Rāma. Hanumāna, Puṣkala, and the minister Sumati lay prostrate at the feet of the sage. When he saw the sacrificial horse protected by the great personage none other than Hanumāna, he said that Rāma alone is the giver of lasting happiness. Meditation on his name destroys the sins and purifies the soul. The divine image of Śrī Rāma Candra and Hanumāna in his heart sent him into ecstasy. He embraced Śatrughna and Hanumāna, one after the other.

There was a kingdom, Devapura, on the bank of Kṣiprā. The ruler of that kingdom was Vīramaṇi. He was a devotee of Mahākāla Śiva. The horse of Aśwamedha reached Devpura. Lord Śiva had assured him, the ruler Vīrmaṇi, that he would protect him till the time a sacrificial horse of Aśwamedha performed by Śrī Rāma reached his state and a battle would be fought. In the fray appeared Vīrasingha, the brother of Vīramaṇi. Hanumāna hit him with his fist at his chest. He fell unconscious. The nephews of Vīrasiṇgha, seeing their uncle falling, came down to fight Hanumāna. How could they stand in the battle? They also fell. Vīrmaṇi tormented Puṣkala, the son of Bharata, in the fight. But Puṣkala shot three arrows at him and he became unconscious. Lord Śiva joined the battle. Vīrbhadra, the chief among his Gaṇas, who was with him, killed Puṣkala. Knowing this Śatrughna fought Lord Śiva. He shot an arrow at the chest of Śatrughna. It pierced into it; he fell unconscious. This angered Hanumāna. Addressing Rudra, he said, "According to hearsay you meditate on the feet of Śrī Rāma. But you have come down to kill the devotees of Rāma. You are defying your own stand. This is against the law of Dharma. I want to punish you for the defiance of Dharma."

Śiva replied, "He was defending his devotees." The reply aggravated Hanumāna. He destroyed the chariot and horses of Lord Śiva. The Lord mounted his Nandi and fought. A fierce battle raged between the two.

Lord Śiva was fighting on both the sides. The battle with Hanumāna exasperated him. He told Hanumāna, "You are a great valorous warrior. I am pleased with you. You ask for a boon."

Hanumāna replied, "Lord! By the grace of Śrī Rāma, I have nothing to ask for. Still I seek that your Gaṇas may protect the body of Puṣkala and the unconscious Śatrughna till I bring Sañjivanī from Droṇagiri."

Lord Śiva consented.

Hanumāna went for the herb, reached the mount, defenders of the mount tried to prevent him. He gave his account. The defenders then permitted him to take the medicinal herb. He brought, administered it and brought Puṣkala back to life, and Śatrughna to consciousness. Hanumāna administered the medicine to all the dying soldiers. They all recovered and stood up to fight.

A fierce battle again raged. Lord Śiva encountered Śatrughna and menaced him. This time Vīrmaṇi fell. This aggravated Lord Śiva further. He raged an attack on Śatrughna. Hanumāna advised to remember Śrī Rāma Candra. He followed the advice. Lord Rāma appeared in the guise of the one performing yajña. He was carrying the horn of a deer in his hand.

Lord Śiva and Śrī Rāma met each other. Śrī Rāma appreciated that Lord Śiva protected his devotees in the battle. He said, "The Gods protect their devotees. This is their tradition. Śiva, you are in my heart and I am in yours; we are, in fact, one."

The warriors of both sides were brought to life. Vīrmaṇi brought the sacrificial horse, ornamented it and presented it to Śatrughna.

Rest of his life he dedicated to the service of the Lord Rāma. So did his sons and the members of his family. This pleased Hanumāna immensely.

The sacrificial horse reached a dense forest on the mount Hemakūṭa. All of a sudden its body became stiff. It could not move its limbs. Śatrughna could not understand the cause. He advised his lieutenants to search for a sage who knew both the past and the future. Such a sage was found out. He was Śaunaka.

Śaunaka revealed that in olden times a Brāhmaṇa had committed some mistake and angered the sages. They cursed him to become a demonic spirit. He prayed for redemption. The sages told, "When you stiffen the body of the sacrificial horse of Śrī Rāma and get an opportunity to listen to his deeds, you would be absolved of the curse and get redeemed." Thus the sage Śaunak advised Śatrughna to go to the horse and narrate the stories of the deeds and acts of Śrī Rāma. Śatrughna followed the advice.

Hearing the deeds of Śrī Rāma, the demonic spirit got redemption.

The horse regained mobility.

The horse reached a place called Kuṇḍalapura. It was ruled over by Suratha. He was a devotee of Śrī Rāma. He was extremely virtuous and defender of dharma. Yama had granted him a boon that he would die only after he got a vision of Śrī Rāma and that he would ever remain free of the fear of death.

Suratha ordered that the horse be made captive. It was duly caught.

Śatrughna dispatched Aṅgada with the message that the horse be released. Suratha made it clear to him that he would not release the horse unless he received the vision of Śrī Rāma. Or, Hanumāna, the valorous, might bind him and secure the release of the horse.

Aṅgada returned with the reply. A battle ensued.

Suratha pitted his ten sons and a large army against that of Śatrughna.

Campaka, one son of Suratha, made Puṣkala his captive.

Hanumāna attacked Campaka. But he remembered Śrī Rāma and aborted the attack. This infuriated Hanumāna jī. He lifted him by the leg and pitted him down on the earth with such force that he got wounded and became unconscious.

Suratha came forward. He cautioned Hanumāna jī that he was to bind him and take him as a captive to his town. Both exchanged some sentences in praise of Śrī Rāma which pleased both of them. But a battle was a battle.

Suratha flourished his bow. Hanumāna jī caught that and broke it into pieces. Suratha took out another; same thing happened to this also. In this way Suratha lost eighty bows.

Suratha shot the Brahmāstra. Hanumāna swallowed it. Lastly, he shot the Rāmāstra. Hanumāna honoured that and was taken captive.

Suratha taunted that Hanumāna should prepare and try for his release.

Hanumāna noted that all the warriors of his side were made captive.

He prayed to his Lord Rāma that his name redeems the gravest sinners. He had liberated many in previous time. This time also he should come down to rescue him.

Śrī Rāma heard the prayer. He descended on the town, reached the place of Hanumāna's captivity. Sporting the four-armed figure, the Lord granted the vision to Suratha. He praised his firmness in adherence to the Dharma of Kṣhatrīya.

All the warriors including Hanumāna were released. The dead were brought back to life.

King Suratha felt exhilarated at thc outcome.

Battle with Lava and Kuśa

The horse reached the vicinity of the hermitage of Vālmīki. Sītā was in the Āśrama. Her two sons Lava and Kuśa were learning the Rāmāyaṇa with the sage. When the horse was roaming there, the children had gone to the forest to gather wood for the fire of yagya. They sighted the horse, got curious and caught it. They brought it to the Āśrama and tied it with a rope to a tree.

Śatrughna was leading the army having all the four wings. He deputed the commander of the army to secure the release of the horse from the possession of the children. Kālajit fought with valour but lay dead in the field due to the tormenting shower of arrows of Lava. The force retreated. But Lava continued fighting.

The son of Bharata, Puṣkala by name, also died at the hands of Lava. Hanumāna jī plunged into the fray. He attacked with boulders and tree trunks. Lava reduced them into small particles. Hanumāna jī surrounded the boy with his tail and sprang up into the sky. Lava remembered his mother and hit the tail with his fists. The attack by fists menaced Hanumāna intensely. Lava secured his release. The attack with arrows turned Hanumāna jī unconscious.

Śatrughna came forward. His arrows wounded Lava. He became unconscious. Śatrughna captured him, bound him and put him in his chariot.

The boys of the hermitage carried the tale to Sīta jī. She became nervous. Lava's elder brother Kuśa consoled her and proceeded to the field to secure his brother's release from bondage. Lava noticed his brother, felt encouraged, tried and became free, sprang off the chariot and began shooting arrows. Kuśa from the Eastern side and Lava from the Western side gave a fierce fight to the army. Kuśa made Śatrughna unconscious. Surath came forward. He also became unconscious due to the attack of Kuśa.

Hanumāna felt aggravated. He engaged Lava. Uprooting a śāla tree, he rushed and attacked him with that. Lava remembered his mother and shot a deadly arrow at Hanumāna. Hanumāna could not withstand it and fell to it.

The army started fleeing. Kush shot Varuṇapāsa at Sugrīva who had come to contain his fleeing army. Sugrīva fell and came under bondage.

Lava and Kuśa bound Hanumāna and Sugrīva tight and brought them into the audience of their revered mother thinking that they were a good source of entertainment.

Sītā viewed them both under bondage, felt sorry. Admonishing her sons, she told them that they were reverable fighters of the Army of Śrī Rāma. Pointing towards them, she said he was Hanumāna who burnt Laṅkā down to ashes and he, Sugrīva, was the king of the monkey clan.

Lava and Kuśa innocently informed their mother that some arrogant monarch of Ayodhyā, named Rāma, the son of some Daśaratha, was performing a sacrificial yagya as a part of which that horse would roam about in various lands. Whoever dared to catch the horse would have to fight the army under Śatrughna.

As true Kśhatrīyas, we did our duty. We vanquished the army of Rāma. Now as you say, we return the horse to its keepers.

Sītā jī prayed to bring the soldiers back to life. They all returned to life.

Sīta enquired of Hanumāna, who recognised her, how a warrior like him could suffer a defeat at the hands of children as they were. Hanumāna humbly said that the father himself had become his son or sons. Your sons are no one other than my master Śrī Rāma. How can I suffer a defeat at my master's hands?

There are very many anecdots about Hanumāna jī. These are told by the story tellers with great interest.

Hanumāna as Rudra

Once Sītā desired to experience the joy of preparing various dishes for Hanumāna. She prepared the dishes and invited him to partake of the food.

Hanumāna sat down to partake. Sīta jī served him with the dishes. He went on eating. The entire quantity of the food she had prepared was finished. But Hanumāna went on asking for more and more. The situation worried her. She remembered her Lord, Śrī Rāma. She visualised that Lord Śaṅkara Himself was taking food in the form of Hanumāna. How could the hunger of Śiva, who destroys thc three worlds at the time of the great annihilation and contains the whole of it within his tummy, could be satiated with that amount of food that Sītā had prepared?

Sītā went at the back of Hanumana, scribed at thc hind of the head Om Namah Śivāya and muttered the prayer, "Please be satiated". Within no time be was satiated.

This relates to the Dwāpara era.

Pāṇḍavas were passing their time in exile. Arjuna had come to Himalayan mountain to propitiate Lord Śaṅkara and to obtain from him some divine weapons for use in the war against the Kauravas.

Bhīmasena with Draupadī and brothers came to the sacred āśrama of Śrī Nara and Nārāyaṇa. When Bhīmasena and Draupadī were roaming the woods, a huge lotus flower of almost one thousand petals came down flying with the wind from Īśana angle and fell where Draupadī was standing. Its fragrance was exceedingly sweet and captivating. She fell in love with it. She beseeched Bhīmasena to obtain any how another flower of the same species so that she could plant it in Kāmyakvana in a pond at her hermitage.

In order to please her and gain her favour, he at once left in the direction from which the flower had landed.

Having covered some distance, he arrived at a vast plantain forest where Hanumāna jī lived. By the roar that Bhīmasena was producing, Hanumāna jī inferred that he was his brother Bhīmasena. Thinking that traversing the forest through the narrow path was not proper and safe for him, he lay across the path to prevent his going.

Bhīmasena pleaded with him to give way. But, he would not, saying that was not meant for humans to traverse.

Repeated negations by Hanumāna jī exasperated Bhīmasena intensely. Ultimately, Hanumāna jī impelled him to lift up his tail and exit if he was so keen to go that way. Bhīma tried repeatedly but could not budge his tail even a little. Perspiring because of hard labour and wiping the streams of sweat off his forehead he enquired about the identity of the great soul. About himself he gave out that he was Pāṇdava of Kuntī and Pāṇdu of the Kurus from the lunar clan of the Kśatrīyas.

Hanumāna jī revealing his identity apprised him of his parentage: son of the God of Wind and Añjanā, the wife of Kesarī of the monkey clan. Then he narrated his deeds and achievements in the battles between Rāma and Rāvaṇa. He also made it clear to him that it was he who had crossed the hundred yojana wide ocean in one jump, to reach Laṅkā where Sīta jī, the spouse of Śrī Rāma, was kept in captivity by Rāvaṇa. He revealed that there were very many supernatural deeds that he had accomplished in the service of his Lord Śrī Rāma.

Bhīmasena then besought him to reveal that form which he had assumed while crossing the ocean. Hanumāna assumed the form that covered the entire plantain forest and rose up beyond the height of the mountain around.

Bhīmasena touched his feet and lay prostrate before him in obeisance. Hanumāna jī, addressing him as brother, proposed that he would bind Duryodhana alongwith his brothers and bring them all to his feet if he so desired. He also put forth to ask for a boon. Bhīmasena replied that his compassionate attitude towards him was all that was needed. The enemy would suffer a defeat in every case.

Still Hanumāna gave out that he was his younger brother and that he would increase the magnitude of his roar many folds when he would penetrate into the formations and arrays of the enemy forces. That roar would deprive the enemy of their life force and he would be able to kill them with no effort.

"Besides, I will occupy a seat on the flag of Arjuna. From there I will terrorise the enemy forces to the degree that they will lose the courage and the will to fight."

Having said thus, Hanumāna jī disappeared from the sight of Bhīmasena.

Hanumāna the Unique

Hanumāna is the noblest and the mightiest character in Hindu mythology. He is the humblest, the purest, the most lovable, the most adorable, the most docile, the most disciplined and the most selfless. He has no personal interest to pursue. He exists only for Rāma and for those who are for Rāma, who love Rāma and whom Rāma loves. Leaving Rāma, he has nothing and nobody to think of. It is rather next to impossible to count his qualities and describe his character in words. There is no mind, human or superhuman, which can fathom the depth or imagine the vastness of the ocean that Hanumāna jī is. Did anyone with whom he interacted—be he Śrī Rāma or Lakṣmaṇa or Sugrīva, or Aṅgada, or Rāvaṇa or the sages—know him fully or completely?

Hanumāna became instrumental in the destruction of the ego in many cases. He did not harbour an iota of this ego in his mind or heart.

Sudarśana Chkra, the weapon, harboured an ego for the reason that it had defeated the thunder bolt of Indra. Also, it thought that his Lord remembered it in difficulty and it came down always to his help.

Garuda, the vehicle of the Lord, too had developed an ego thinking that it had a terrible speed, carried his Lord on his back, tormented the demons with its bill, the wings and the claws.

Satyabhāma also thought that she was the most beautiful woman in the three worlds and wanted to know if Sītā was more beautiful than her. She obviously harboured an ego.

Lord Kṛṣṇa (Rāma of Tretā and Kṛṣṇa of Dwāpara) called Hanumāna to teach all the three how to get rid of ego that was troubling them.

Hanumāna the monkey appeared in the well protected woods of the palaces of Dwāraka. He started destroying the beauty of the garden. The matter was reported to Lord Kṛṣṇa. He summoned Garuḍa and told him to carry the army with him to instruct the monkey in the ways of decent living.

Garuḍa felt humiliated at the command of taking the army with him to deal with a monkey when he had fought battles with demons, but did not speak against the command. It approached the monkey and tried to admonish him for misdeeds in the garden. Hanumāna did not take him seriously. Garuḍa tried to attack him. Hanumāna surrounded Garuḍa with his tail. It felt helpless as an insignificant bird would do. It cited the name of Śrī Kṛṣṇa in its favour. Hanumāna replied with the name of Lord Rāma. This infuriated Garuḍa. Hanumāna jī did not want to hurt it seriously. He caught its wings and threw it into the sea nearby. Garuḍa fell into the water, was nearly drowned, drank some amount of sea water, lost consciousness a bit and recovered after some time, its ego set aright. When it returned to the court of Kṛṣṇa, its body was drenched. The Lord asked sarcasticaly if it had a sea wash. It said, "The monkey was extraordinary. He threw me into the sea".

Hanumāna jī had gone to Malayagiri after the episode. Kṛṣṇa realised that he was none other than Hanumāna.

Now to set it aright further, he ordained that it should go to Hanumāna and fetch him from Malayagiri where he had gone after the encounter with him. Let Hanumāna be told that Śrī Rāma wanted him. Garuḍa duly left.

He asked Satyabhāma to sit beside him in the form of Sītā jī. He also told her that Hanumāna loved Rāma and Sītā jī only. Kṛṣṇa also deployed Sudarśana to protect Dwārkā and ordered that it should not allow entry to anybody.

Garuḍa reached Hanumāna and asked him to come to Dwārakā as Śrī Rāma Candra wanted him in Dwārakā.

Hanumāna told Garuḍa to leave saying that he would follow and reach soon.

Garuḍa felt indignant at the reply. It flew with a confidence of speed and strength in its wings.

Hanumāna reached Dwārakā before Garuḍa could reach. At the precincts of Dwārakā, he was prevented by the Sudarśana Chakra. Hanumāna caught hold of the Chakra and made him captive in his mouth. Hanumāna entered the palace, presented himself at the feet of Śrī Rāma Candra and enquired where mother Sītā jī was. He also enquired who that maid servant was sitting beside him. Satyabhāma felt ashamed.

Śrī Kṛṣṇa in the form of Śrī Rāma enquired if he was prevented from entering the palace by anybody. Hanumāna replied that the Sudarśana Chakra was detaining him at the gate. That was the reason he had kept that in his mouth. With these words, he took out the Chakra Sudarśana and placed it at the feet of the Lord. The Chakra was freed from his captivity.

He had destroyed the ego of Arjuna also when the Dwāpara era was nearing its end.

Arjuna once boasted that he could build a bridge with his arrows. This he said when Hanumāna had said that he was one of the monkeys who had built the bridge across the sea for the army of monkeys and bears to cross over to Laṅkā.

Hanumāna said that the bridge of arrows would have given way under the weight of the monkeys.

Arjuna did not accept the argument. He constructed a bridge with the arrows. Hanumāna set his thumb over it and it crumbled.

Arjuna and his knowledge of archery got humiliated. Arjuna could not bear it. He had taken a vow that if anybody insulted his archery, he would burn himself down on a pyre.

So, he prepared a pyre. When he was going to burn himself down, a Brahmacārī appeared and asked for the cause.

Arjuna narrated the incident and told him the cause.

The Brahmacārī came out with the counter argument that there was no witness in the dispute.

He asked to re-enact the episode. Arjuna re-built the bridge with arrows. Hanumāna first placed his thumb over it and sat down on it casting his whole weight over it. The bridge did not crumble then. Thus the life of Arjuna was saved.

Hanumāna said that Arjuna was saved by the Brahmacārī who had given his support under the bridge. Śrī Kṛṣṇa had supported the bridge from beneath it with the help of his Chakra. Hanumāna had the vision of the Lord Kṛṣṇa. Kṛṣṇa embraced him.

The Lord always saves his devotees. Hanumāna had saved the chariot of Arjuna in the battle of Mahābhārata. Kṛṣṇa had made it clear to Arjuna. Hanumāna is defender of the devotees of the Lord.

Hanumāna had destroyed the ego of Śani also. Once he had challenged Hanumāna for a dual. Hanumāna encircled him with his tail. He felt helpless. Hanumāna ran with Śani bound in his tail, over the rocks and mounts. Śani prayed for his release soon. Hanumāna took the promise that he would never transfer his evil effect onto a devotee of Śrī Rāma. Śani gave the promise and secured his release.

The qualities of Hanumāna lie beyond description; his character is beyond the power of mind. He is, in fact, beyond comprehension.

Appendix

Some valuable verses from various sources which exemplify the might and courage of Hanumāna.

उल्लड़्.ध्य सिन्धोः सलिलम् सलीलम्,
यः शोक वह्निं जनकात्मजायाः
आदाय तेनैव ददाह लड़्.काम्,
नमामि तं प्रा जलि रा जनेयम्।।

ullaṅghya sindhoḥ: salilam salīlam,
ya: śokavahniṁ janakātmajāyā:
ādāya tenaiva dadāha Laṅkām,
namāmi taṁ prāñjalirāñjaneyam

I pray with my folded hands and rever Hanumāna jī, the progeny of mother Añjanā, who crossed the vast expanse of water of the sea, reached Laṅkā, took the fire of the agony of the daughter of Janaka and burnt the whole town to ashes.

मनोजवं मारूततुल्य वेगम्
जितेन्द्रियम् बुद्धिमताम् वरिष्ठम्।
वातात्मजम् वानरयूथ मुख्यम्,
श्रीरामदूतम् शिरसा नमामि।।

Manojavaṁ mārutatulya vegam,
Jitendriyam buddhimatām variṣṭhaṁ,
Vātātmajaṁ vānarayūtha mukhyaṁ,
Šrīrāmadūtaṁ sirasā namāmi

I bow my head in reverence to the messenger of Śrī Rāma, the progeny of the God of Wind, the foremost in the troops of the monkeys, the master of his senses, the greatest among the erudite, who equalled his progenitor in the matter of speed and who could move as fast as the mind.

अतुलितबलधामम् हैमशैलाभदेहम्,
दनुजवनक शानुम ज्ञानिनामग्रगण्यम।
सकलगुणनिधानम् वानराणामधीशम्,
रघुपति प्रियभक्तम् वातजातम् नमामि।

Atulitabaladhāmaṁ haimašeilābhadehaṁ,
Danujavanakṛšānum jňāninamagragaṇyam,
Sakalaguṇanidhānam vānarāṇamadhīšam
Raghupatipriyabhaktiam vātajātaṁ namami

I rever the offspring of the God of Wind, the dear devotee of the scion of the lineage of Raghu, the commander of the troops of the monkeys, the abode of all the good qualities, the foremost among the learned, endowed with wisdom, the burning flame for the forest of the demonic evil spirits, whose body gleans like the mount of gold and who is the abode of the immeasurable light.

यत्र यत्र रघुनाथ कीर्तनम् तत्र तत्र क तमस्तका जलिम,
वाष्पवारि परिपूर्ण लोचनम्, मारूतिम् नमत राक्षसान्तकम्।।

yatra-yatra raghunātha kīrtanaṁ,
tatra-tatra kṛtamastkāñjaliṁ,
vaṣpavāri paripūrṇa locanaṁ,
mārutiṁ namata r̄akṣasāntakam

Where the name of the Lord of the lineage of Raghu Śrī Rāma is sung, Hanumāna bows his head there in obeisance to him, his eyes brimming with tears; May you all salute him, the destroyer of the demons.

Hanumāna's Might :

लड़.धयित्वा जलनिधिम् क त्वा लड़.का च भस्म सात्।।
रावणम् सकुलम् हत्वा नेष्ये जनकनन्दिनीम्।
यद्वा बद्ध्वा गले रज्वा रावणम् वामपाणिना।।
लड़.काम् सपर्वताम् घ त्वा रामस्याग्रे क्षिपाम्यहम्।
यद्वा द ष्ट्वैव यास्यानि जानकीं शुभलक्षणाम्।।

Laṅghayitā jalanidhim kṛtvā laṅkaiñca bhasmasāt
Rāvaṇam sakulam hatvā SS neṣye janaka nandinīṁ
Yadvā badhvā gale rajvā rāvaṇaṁ vāmpāṇinā
Laṅkāṁ saparvtām ghritvā rāmasyāgre kshipāmyaham
Yadva driṣṭyaiva yāsyāni jānakīṁ šubhlakṣṇām

Having crossed the sea, reduced the whole of Laṅkā to ashes, wiped out Rāvaṇa with his kith and kin, I can bring the daughter of Janaka, endowed with all the auspicious features. Or, roping Rāvaṇa in neck by my left hand and lifting Laṅkā with the mounts on which it is situated I may throw at the feet of Rāma. Or, I may be detailed as to whether I should view her only and return.

यद्वा राघवनिर्मुक्तः शरः श्वसन विक्रमः
गच्छेत् तद्वद् गमिष्यामि लड़्.काम् रावणपालिताम्।
नहि द्रक्ष्यामि यदि तां लड़्.कायाम् जनकात्मजाम्।।
अनेनैव हि वेगेन गमिष्यामि सुरालयम्।
यदि वा त्रिदिवे सीताभ् न द्रक्ष्यामि क तश्र मः।।
बद्ध्वा राक्षसराजानमानयिष्यामि रावणम्।
सर्वथा क तकार्यो हमेष्यामि सह सीतया।।
आनयिष्यामि वा लड़्.काम् समुत्पाट्य सरावणाम्।

yadvā rāghavanirmuktaḥ šaraḥ švasanvikramaḥ
gacchet tadvad gamiṣyāmi Laṅkām rākṣasapālitāṁ
nahi drakṣyāmi yadi tām laṅkāyām janakātmajām,
aneneiva hi vegena gamiṣyāmi surālayam,
yadva tridive sītam na drkṣyami kṛtašrama
baddhvā rakṣaso rājānamānay iṣyāmi rāvaṇaṁ
sarvathā kṛtakaryosham eṣyāmi saha sītayā
ānayiṣyāmi vā laṅkām samutpāṭya sarāvaṇām,

I will go as the arrow shot by Śrī Rāma flies with the speed of the wind and reach Laṅkā. If I do not see her there, I will proceed to the heaven with that very speed; if I do not perceive her there and my labour does not produce result, I will rope Rāvaṇa down and bring him here as a captive. I will return successful with Sītā jī or I will uproot Laṅkā off its foundation and bring it here down with Rāvaṇa.

[Va. Ra. 5-1-39 to 43]